THE GREAT CENTRAL
IN LNER DAYS 2

David Jackson & Owen Russell

LONDON

IAN ALLAN LTD

First published 1986

ISBN 0 7110 1612 7

Published by Ian Allan Ltd,
Shepperton, Surrey; and printed
by Ian Allan Printing Ltd at their
works at Coombelands in
Runnymede, England

Front cover:
'Director' Class D11 4-4-0 No 5505 *Ypres* **and
'Sandringham' Class B17 4-6-0 No 2816** *Fallodon* **near
Preston Road with the 3.20pm Marylebone-Manchester i**
1935. *F. R. Hebron/Rail Archive Stephenson*

Below:
Symbol of an era. 'B3' No 6165 *Valour* **was one of the
best-known of all Gorton-designed engines, and very
much a part of the GC section scene in the years covered
by this book. It is seen standing at the north end of
Nottingham Victoria station in the late 1930s.**
J. N. Hall/Rail Archive Stephenson

Contents

Preface

This book may be regarded as a companion volume to 'The Great Central in LNER Days' (Ian Allan Ltd 1983), and in it we have adopted the same approach to the subject of locomotives and traffic on the former Great Central Railway system. On this occasion however we have taken the opportunity of going into greater detail than last time, and with the same overall length of text as previously this has resulted in fewer chapters. In making this more restricted selection of material we have nevertheless attempted as before to preserve a balance in the subjects dealt with, and we offer chapters covering express passenger working as well as the much more neglected themes of local passenger, fast goods and mineral traffic. Likewise we have tried to make our selection as wide as possible from a geographical point of view, and our story includes references to most of the main centres of Great Central section traffic, as well as certain parts of the Great Northern and Great Eastern. As before, the information presented is in the main completely original, and to the best of our knowledge has never been previously published except, in certain cases, in articles of our own authorship.

It is our dearest wish that some of the scenes we have tried to describe (reconstructed principally from conversations, documents and photographs) will be recognisable to at least some of those readers old enough to remember the inter-war era. We also take this opportunity of thanking all those who so kindly wrote to us expressing their appreciation of The Great Central in LNER Days, and we humbly hope that the present volume will not fall too far below it in quality.

As for such views or opinions as may be occasionally expressed in the text, it goes without saying that these are founded on evidence that has come to hand, whether in printed or oral form, over a very lengthy period of research, and are not the product of preconceived ideas of our own. We readily take full responsibility for what is said, and we will always be glad to hear from readers who might wish to add to or alter the story in any way.

Acknowledgements
We could never have attempted to write a book such as this without seeking the assistance of a large number of individuals, and the task of acknowledging their help, in every case freely and willingly given, is not an easy one. Pride of place naturally goes to the many railwaymen who over the years have readily allowed themselves to be subjected to a barrage of questions, and it is from their answers that much of the content of this book has been compiled. They are far too numerous to mention individually, but we take this welcome opportunity of making particular mention of several who are now no longer with us, and to whom the book may in its small way be regarded as a tribute. They are Bill Botham, Charlie Clough, Ron Eagles, George Hutson, Eddie Jubb, Frank Rushton, Bert Wagstaff and George White.

Others who have helped us in a variety of ways include Messrs C. A. Appleton, J. F. Aylard, D. S. Barrie, H. D. Bowtell, W. A. Brown, A. Y. Bryant, T. Butcher, J. Chorlton, G. Dow, F. Hallam, R. H. N. Hardy, K. Hoole, J. Hosegood, K. Jones, W. G. Kirby, G. Knight, K. A. Ladbury, B. Longbone, D. Mason, H. Middleton, R. T. Munns, Miss E. Naylor, E. Neve, the late W. Nock, E. Payne, R. C. Riley, R. E. Rose, D. Rowland, Mrs. P. Shaw, B. Stephenson, R. G. C. Stephenson, W. Tagg, D. H. Yarnell, W. B. Yeadon, and various members of the Severn Valley Railway Society.

We also take the opportunity of mentioning the GCR Society, our joint membership of which has proved of immense value in a variety of ways, and some parts of the material included in this and our previous title first saw the light of day in the Society's magazine *Forward*.

To all who helped us in any way, great or small, our sincere thanks.

D. J. and O. R.

Below:
A typical Eason's excursion of the 1930s. 'B7' No 5467 of Immingham is seen at New Southgate with an up excursion on Saturday 20 May 1933.
E. R. Wethersett/Rail Archive Stephenson

I

The 'North Country Continental'

' . . . at Ipswich, our Parkeston engine came off, and to take us on we have a "Sandringham". This is a Gorton engine and it will take us right through to Manchester Central . . . '

R. Barnard Way, *Mixed Traffic*

It was 1937 when R. Barnard Way made his journey in the guard's van of the 'North Country Continental', and at that date the train was at the height of its fame. Though never to achieve even a fraction of the publicity which surrounded such expresses as the 'Flying Scotsman' or 'Queen of Scots', and by 1937 pushed even further into the background with the advent of the much-celebrated streamlined trains, the 'North Country Continental' remained, from a locomotive working point of view if from no other, a most unusual train. This is how the late Cecil J. Allen described it:

'One of the most remarkable through cross-country locomotive workings in the country was made by this train, for a three-cylinder 4-6-0 of the B17 or 'Sandringham' Class took it over at Ipswich and worked it right through for 216 miles to Manchester – a continuous journey of 5¾ hours with unchanged engine crew, varying in characteristics from the extraordinary flatness of the Fen Country to an altitude of all but 1,000 feet above the sea on entering Woodhead Tunnel, and from the quietude of a single-line country branch to the teeming manufacturing areas of Sheffield and Manchester.[1]

Few better descriptions could be given. This was a daily performance in both directions, except for Sundays, and if the reader pauses to wonder at the comparatively modest fame which the train has gained in railway literature, the answer probably lies in the rather out-of-the-way route which it followed; this is shown on the accompanying sketch-plan. The 'Continental' was a creature of the railway byways, and in addition to the absence of publicity it is hardly surprising to learn that the

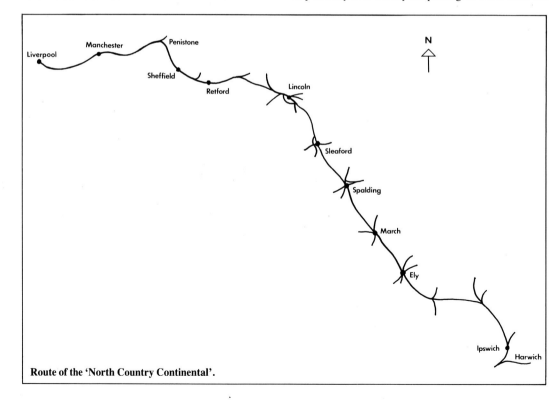

Route of the 'North Country Continental'.

number of photographs of it is very small compared, for instance, with the expresses which used the Kings Cross-Edinburgh main line.

This is all the more curious when it is recalled that the train was associated with some extremely interesting locomotive developments, particularly in connection with Class B17. It was almost certainly on the 'Continental', for example, that the pioneer engines of this class performed their very first revenue-earning duties in late 1928, and during the following decade the 'Continental' saw the first regular use of the new 'Footballer' series of 'B17s' over former GER metals; so little publicity did these events receive that neither has been recorded in the best-authenticated history of the class.[2] But all this is to anticipate the story, and to begin at the beginning we must go back to a time before the 'B17s' had been built, and before through working between Manchester and Ipswich had ever been thought of.

In pre-Grouping days the 'North Country Continental' had been a joint venture between the Great Central and Great Eastern Railways, with the latter originally being the senior partner on account of its ownership of the shipping facilities. The main train plied between York and the terminal at Harwich, with a portion attached at Lincoln conveying passengers from Liverpool and Manchester, and similar arrangements operating in the opposite direction. By Grouping however this situation had altered considerably. The main train now went to Manchester and Liverpool, probably reflecting the increased custom generated in the more populous northwest, and passengers for York were now accommodated in a portion which was detached at Sleaford and worked via Honington to Grantham where it was put on to a down main line express; this portion was also advertised as a through service to Glasgow. The up Glasgow portion ran via Sheffield, and was attached there.

The distinguishing characteristic of the 'Continental' in early LNER days, in sharp contrast to the situation described by R. Barnard Way, was the large number of engine changes made in the course of each journey. As the up train wended its somewhat leisurely way forward from Merseyside to the Suffolk coast, it must have seemed to the interested traveller that a fresh engine was waiting to take over at every call. On the Great Central section, engine-changes were made at Manchester Central, Sheffield and Lincoln, and involved engines from Trafford Park, Gorton and Lincoln Locos. The train was handed over to the GE section at Lincoln, the traditional frontier-post between the Great Central and Great Eastern Railways, and further changes of engine would be made at March and Ipswich before the train finally found itself on the quayside at Harwich. Similar arrangements applied in the opposite direction, and the use of six engines to work a train over not much more than 270 miles was probably something of a record. In 1925 however the GER section cut out engine-changing altogether in the down direction and diagrammed a Parkeston and Ipswich engines, usually a 'B12', to take the train through to Lincoln, though with a change of crew en route.

At this period therefore the 'Continental' could claim considerable interest from a locomotive point of view, with a good variety of both Great Central and Great Eastern engines to be seen along the route. On the Liverpool-Manchester section, Trafford Park almost invariably used 'D6' 4-4-0s, a type which then, and for a good many years afterwards, had an almost complete monopoly of the main passenger trains on this part of the Cheshire Lines Committee. They were known to one and all in that part of the world as 'Pollitts', and were highly popular with the enginemen. The up and down 'Continenal' turns were operated as part of two separate diagrams, both typical of the many express workings which Trafford Park Loco handled between Manchester and Liverpool. In the up direction 40 minutes were allowed, and five minutes more the other way; departure from Liverpool was at 2.30 and the down train got in at three o'clock, the two trains passing each other in the vicinity of Halewood.

Gorton were responsible for the Manchester-Sheffield section, using Class B2 engines in both directions. At this early period all six of the class were stationed at Gorton and worked in the No 2 Link, which mainly involved trips to Sheffield and back; the 'B2s' were very popular with their crews, and were known as 'City' class engines. The down working was highly typical of the No 2 Link as it was at that period, the engine leaving London Road station at 10.03am on a Cleethorpes express which it relinquished at Sheffield to return on the Continental, due out at 12.50. In the other direction the diagram was subject to seasonal variations: normally the 'Continental' left Manchester Central at 3.18 with coaches for Cleethorpes included in the train, but on busy Saturdays the two ran separately, the 'Continental' then departing at 3.22. When the normal departure was in force the Gorton engine is understood to have worked through to Retford with the Cleethorpes portion, returned to Sheffield on a stopping train arriving at 6.50 and finally arriving home on the 8.27 departure from the latter, which was a through Hull-Manchester train. When the 'Continental' left at 3.22 the engine worked to Sheffield only and had a straightforward return on the 6.10pm departure, a summer-season train from Cleethorpes to Manchester London Road. During the 1925 season the latter arrangement is known to have operated throughout the week as well as on Saturdays, and may have done so in 1926. Unfortunately no notes of these early Gorton workings appear to have survived, but it is known that on Armistice Days the 10.03am diagram was performed by No 6165 *Valour*, as described later in this book.[3]

Lincoln covered the next leg of the trip, using yet another variety of Gorton-designed passenger engine. The 'D9' 4-4-0s, as they had now become under the LNER, are generally considered to have been amongst the most handsome of GCR four-coupled types. Painted LNER green at this period and still retaining their original ornate brasswork they looked very much their best, and the Lincoln-based engines were kept in sparkling condition for the 'Continental' working, which was their main duty. The diagram was neatly arranged so that they left Lincoln on the down train at 11.36am, turned at Sheffield and came back on the up train to reach Lincoln again at 5.43pm, the whole working slotting conveniently into a single shift and requiring only one engine and crew. During the week an extra trip was fitted in at Sheffield, the engine running light to Orgreave and returning with a workmen's train due in Sheffield at 2.50pm. This arrangement did not operate on Saturdays, and instead there was a turn to Penistone and back with stopping passenger trains, leaving Sheffield at 2.25pm and getting back at 4.04pm. The humble nature of these fill-in turns was something of a come-down for the highly burnished 'D9', but probably excited little comment at Sheffield as in those days there was a large fleet of the class at Neepsend Loco employed on all kinds of work including the unglamorous miners' trains.

Top Link men were in charge of the 'Continental' diagram at Lincoln Loco, and by 1925 the turn was being shared between the two senior passenger drivers, Ralph Thompson and George Emmett, using engines Nos 5113, 6018 and 6021. There is a report that a Great Northern 4-4-0, 'D2' No 4369, was used on the 'Continental' turn for a time in late 1926, but the newcomer does not seem to have lasted long and was no doubt unpopular with the GCR men, used to the much stronger 'D9'.

East of Lincoln, the working of the 'Continental' was usually entrusted to 'B12s' and 'Claud Hamilton' 4-4-0s, with 'D13s' occasionally deputising for the latter at March Loco. The Great Eastern section workings of this early period fall to some extent outside the scope of this book, but it is interesting that from about the summer of 1925 a through working was introduced in the down

direction, as described earlier, which took a 'B12' 4-6-0 right through from Harwich to Lincoln, remanned en route. The diagram was a somewhat complicated one, with Parkeston and Ipswich engines working the duty on alternate days, but it may be regarded perhaps as a harbinger of things to come.

The great change which overtook the 'North Country Continental' in May 1927 was a twofold one, affecting both engine workings and public timetables. The changes in schedule principally affected the up train, which was now retimed to leave Liverpool 25 minutes earlier for a correspondingly earlier arrival at Parkeston Quay. Also, the through connection from York and the north was altered to join the main train at Lincoln, thus doing away with the long wait at Sheffield. In the opposite direction the York portion was re-timetabled to come off at Lincoln instead of Sleaford, and the whole service now closely resembled that of pre-Grouping days when the GER had worked the main portion through from Harwich to York. All these changes came into effect on Saturday 14 May.

The changes in working were comprehensive to a degree. Except for the Liverpool-Manchester section, the arrangements described earlier were completely done away with, and in their place came through engine working between Manchester and Ipswich. Crews from Gorton and Ipswich sheds were now scheduled to work through over the whole distance and to lodge on a three-nights-weekly basis, making outward trips on Mondays, Wednesdays and Fridays and returning on Tuesdays, Thursdays and Saturdays. Such lengthy forays into 'foreign' territory were up to then completely unknown at the two sheds involved; Gorton men had never penetrated further east than Lincoln, and, apart from an odd working along the GER joint line, Ipswich men were restricted to routes south of March. Both sets of crews therefore had a considerable stretch of new road to learn before the workings could commence, and this is thought to have been done at the beginning of May. Through running is understood to have begun on the Monday following the changes in schedule, which was 16 May.

Although lodging at a place as far afield as Ipswich was a new experience for the Gorton men, the regular habit of lodging on the through London turns meant that the new working was something less of a novelty for them than for their colleagues in East Anglia, among whom lodging was largely unknown. The mileage also corresponded closely with the London turns, being 215 per trip compared with 212 miles from Manchester Central to Marylebone. At Gorton the Ipswich men were introduced to lodging in the true Great Central style, with the barracks and its attendant facilities provided for their use. Gorton men visiting Ipswich were accommodated in private lodgings, usually at No 18 Croft Street, a short walk from the shed.

Because of the important nature of the new workings, they were naturally offered to the senior passenger men at both sheds. At Ipswich two of the then top-flight drivers, George Pinkney and Jack Pack, were assigned to the 'Manchester Job' as it became known, working it between them on alternate trips and filling in the 'off' days with a short-distance turn to Norwich. Both drivers were teamed with a regular fireman, Driver Pinkney working with Ernie Payne and his opposite number with Harry Church.

A different arrangement came into effect at Gorton. The Ipswich lodging turn was rostered to a single crew, Jack Howard and Jack Pomfret, instead of being shared or put into a link. The two were well known to each other, having worked together for some time as the Trial Trip crew, and in opting to take over the Ipswich turn they were exchanging a nine-to-five job for one which involved continual lodging three nights out of every seven, week in and week out. They were of course well remunerated for this inconvenience.

Because of these manning arrangements the 'Continental' was something of an 'odd man out' among Gorton passenger workings, although it should be mentioned that at this period it was not unusual for certain turns to be reserved for individual crews, particularly where specialised road knowledge was involved. It was however necessary to teach another driver the road through to Ipswich in the event of absence of Driver Howard, and the choice is believed to have fallen on David Horne, a senior driver who up to this time had been working on fast goods and fish jobs.

The through 'Continental' working was to have a profound and lasting effect on the express passenger situation at Gorton Loco. In the field of diagramming, the disappearance of the old No 2 Link workings described earlier resulted in a comprehensive restructuring of all the principal workings except the London lodging turns; however, this story falls outside the scope of the present work and must be left for a future occasion. Equally important events took place in the locomotive sphere, and though more delayed in their effect than the diagram changes they can be seen in retrospect to have marked the dawning of a new era at Gorton. The start of all this was a decision as to the type of engine to be used on the through Ipswich runs.

On account of the severe running restrictions which existed at that time on the GE section, Gorton-designed engines were not permitted south of March and were thus out of the reckoning. The situation was such that only ex-GER engines could be used, and of these the only type considered really strong enough for the long-distance working was the 'B12' 4-6-0. In order to ensure that the engines were capable of tackling it, 'B12' No 8561 was tried out during March or April on a Canadian emigrants' special, which it worked through from Ipswich to Liverpool with Jack Pack and Fireman Frank Cocksedge in charge: this showed that in the hands of a good crew the GER 4-6-0 was perfectly able to handle the new working, and so it came about that 'B12' No 8557 was posted to Gorton on 18 April 1927.

The Gorton staff were not unaccustomed to contact with 'foreign' engines, but these were mostly of GNR origin and it is doubtful if they had ever seen a 'B12' any nearer than Lincoln, let alone discovered one standing in the Loco yard. We can do no more than speculate on their reactions, but bearing in mind the strong partisan feelings which existed among Great Central men we may be sure that the newcomer was quickly summed up in a few expressive words, most of them probably not to be found in the Oxford Dictionary. However, even the most critical of onlookers would have taken due note of the engine's solid construction, so much unlike the rather tinny Doncaster products, and when the new crew took charge of her they would be equally pleased with the steady riding, reminiscent of the engines they had grown up with at Gorton. With the new working due to commence on 16 May, as mentioned, Driver Howard and his mate had exactly a month in which to accustom themselves thoroughly to the new machine.

The earliest dated observation of the 'Continental' that has been traced is Saturday 16 July, when 'B12' No 8561 was noted leaving Manchester Central on the up train. Gorton's No 8557 took the train out of Manchester on Wednesday 27 July, and was noted returning from Ipswich on the following Saturday; No 8561 was in charge of the up train on the latter date, and No 8535 likewise on Saturday 3 September. Kept in first-class condition, the original 'B12s' were remarkably consistent performers, as this description by former fireman Ernie Payne makes clear:

'Pinkney had 8535 and Pack 8561. Both ran their engine for over twelve months without losing them on any trip. George Pinkney was Branch Secretary and instructor in the Mutual Improvement Class, and I had been on the "1500s" for nearly two years, so when at work we were "every button on duty" – locomotive work as it should be.'

9

Such consistency could only be achieved by the most meticulous attention and maintenance. Before and after each trip the engines were examined thoroughly, and at both sheds senior cleaners were responsible for getting them ready for the road. Ipswich kept a stock of Rother Vale coal specially reserved for the Manchester engines. In the rare event of a failure there was no suitable stand-by engine available anywhere west of Lincoln, and so it was all the more essential that the engines should be kept well up to concert pitch. Later on, when failures did occasionally occur at the Manchester end, it became the practice for the crew to work as far as Lincoln or March with a Gorton engine, arrangements having been made at one of these places for a GER machine to be provided for the rest of the journey.

In its original form the diagram began in Manchester with the men booking on at 1.05pm and after an hour had been allowed for engine preparation proceeding to Manchester Central for departure at 3.05pm. This part of the diagram was amended later on to incorporate an earlier start from the shed, whence the engine proceeded to Guide Bridge and worked the 1.55pm stopping passenger train to Central, arriving at 2.29pm; this was done to eliminate the unproductive light engine running which at that time was very common on passenger diagrams and which the management gradually sought to do away with in the interests of economy. The slow train was usually worked tender-first so that the engine could couple up to the express without delay after reaching Central. At the Ipswich end a relief crew was waiting at the station to take over the engine so that the main-line men could book off duty and go directly to their lodgings or home as appropriate.

The return working began at Ipswich Loco at 6.30am, and after the usual hour for preparation the engine worked into Ipswich station for a departure at 8.02am. Arrival in Manchester Central was at 2.07pm, the engine then running light to Gorton Loco. Not long after the introduction of the working, however, a change was made whereby the crew were relieved at Guide Bridge, in order to keep their shift within the eight-hour limit. After arriving at Central the relief crew came back to Guide Bridge with the 4.28pm stopping train, whence they took the engine back to Gorton.

The 'B12' engines remained in full charge of the 'Continental' workings for a period of over 18 months, and whatever may have been the early opinions of Gorton men, appear to have performed very creditably. According to one observer they were only just able to tackle the climb to Woodhead on the down journey, but they cannot have been in any serious trouble here

because Fireman Ernie Payne claimed that in the whole of his time on the 'Continental' not a single minute was lost by the engine. Clearly the experience of the crews counted for a good deal, and the fact that the same men were responsible for the working over a long period of time probably contributed a good deal towards the record of consistency. It was common knowledge at Gorton that Jack Howard was not very happy if for any reason he had to work to Ipswich with a different mate, and no doubt something similar could be said of the Ipswich men.

In the spring of 1928 No 8557 was replaced at Gorton by No 8538, no doubt because it was getting due for overhaul after having completed nearly 12 months of regular work on the 'Continental'. Its last known appearance was on Easter Monday, 9 April, when it took out the up train, working opposite No 8535. Its successor appears to have worked with equal consistency throughout the rest of the year, though no precise notes are available. The same standard of reliability was maintained at Ipswich, where over the whole period up to the end of 1928 only four 'B12s' are definitely known to have been used, these being the two originals and Nos 8555 and 8563.

The end of regular 'B12' working was signalled with the arrival at Gorton of No 2802 *Walsingham*, first of the new 'B17' 'Sandringham' class to go into service. The official date of this event was 30 November, but no record has survived of the actual day when this machine first worked the 'Continental'. With engines of several other LNER classes having worked from Gorton not long before, it may well have been supposed at the time that No 2802 was yet another in the procession of Gresley types being tried on the Great Central, none of which had so far lasted very long. In fact the very opposite proved to be the case, because the new class were presently to obtain a firm hold on the GC section, and were to remain part of the scene for many years to come.

Designed to operate almost as widely over the GE section as did the 'B12s', the 'B17s' were a complete contrast in appearance, embodying features which by this time the Gorton staff would recognise as typical of Gresley, notably the cab and controls, the sinuously curved running plates, crescent nameplate and a valve-gear which emitted a musical clank strongly reminiscent of a 'K3'. The total effect was outwardly very pleasing indeed, but the Gorton people were not likely to have set much store by such things as their recent experiences with Gresley machines had given them a strong dislike of anything associated with

Doncaster. They were soon to find that the 'B17s' embodied some of the least pleasant characteristics of Doncaster products, above all a strong tendency to vibrate at speed, which made for very rough riding. As a result the class became unpopular.

Walsingham's first partner on the opposite half of the 'Continental' working was No 2806 *Audley End*, sent to Ipswich early in January 1929, although it appears that at least one trip to Manchester was made by No 2808 *Gunton*, of Stratford shed; no explanation for this unusual appearance can be given. No 2806 was joined on 23 January by No 2807 *Blickling*. Alternating in the same way as the 'B12s' had done, these two settled down to a spell of many years of work on the 'Continental', and in time became as familiar on the Woodhead section as were any Great Central-based engines. Their original opposite number, *Walsingham*, did not last long at Gorton however, being replaced by No 2809 *Quidenham* on 5 March. The reason for this early switch is not known, but in view of the problems shortly to be encountered with engines of this class it may well have been mechanical trouble.

No 2809 remained in Manchester until June 1930, when it was moved away in circumstances shortly to be described. The earliest note of its working that has been traced is Saturday 23 March 1929, when it was in charge of the down train; nearly a month later, on Saturday 20 April, No 2806 *Audley End* was observed on the up working, and was seen again on the same turn on Saturday 1 June.

In about 1929 new sets of LNER-type stock were put into service on the 'Continental', and with the new 'B17s' at the head it was now running in the form which was to become familiar until September 1939. One notable feature of the new coaches was the very long nameboards carried, bearing a variegated list of the numerous places called at en route.

The stock workings were straightforward, with a set of coaches operating from each end on a turn-and-turn-about basis, and a single portion based at Harwich for the daily trip to York and back. After reaching Liverpool at 3pm the coaches of the down train had a short stay in the city before forming the 4pm Liverpool-Hull express; they spent the night in Hull and returned to Liverpool as the 8.55am express from Hull Paragon, arriving in plenty of time for the next 'Continental' working. When not running as a separate train, the Cleethorpes coaches mentioned earlier were detached at Sheffield and taken forward to connect with the afternoon steamer for Germany; they came back next day as part of a Cleethorpes-Manchester express and were worked through to Liverpool in time to join the up 'Continental' again.

During 1930 there were some unexpected happenings in the locomotive sphere. Because of defects traced in the 'B17s' following an accident to No 2808 *Gunton* in October 1929[4], all of the class had to make lengthy visits to Stratford Works for attention to the frames, some of these repairs taking as long as eight months. As a result there were not enough 'B17s' to cover the 'Continental' regularly, and so the trusty 'B12s' came back on the scene. No 8537 was noted on the down train on Monday 3 February 1930, and settled down to a spell of regular work on the 'Continental', at first partnered by No 2807 *Blickling*, and later by another 'B12', No 8577. The latter was seen on the down 'Continental' on Wednesday 30 April, several days before its predecessor *Blickling* entered Stratford Works. After being in Stratford from January, No 2806 *Audley End* returned to the fray on 25 July, its stay of over six months in the works offering a fair example of the extent to which these major repairs interfered with the 'B17s' availability.

At the Gorton end No 2809 *Quidenham* departed from the scene at about the end of May, its last recorded appearance being on the down train on Thursday the 22nd. It was replaced by No 8530, shown in the records as transferred to Gorton on 2 June; previously at Cambridge, it remained in Manchester for only one week before going back to the Great Eastern section again when replaced by another of the class, No 8531. Its short-term transfer suggests a hurried switch to plug an unexpected gap, possibly occasioned by a failure of No 2809 on the road. During its brief spell it was noted working the down train on Tuesday 3 June, while its successor, No 8531, was seen going in the opposite direction just over a week later, on 11 June. The latter continued to operate from Gorton until at least Tuesday 22 July, when it was on the down train, having been noted on several occasions prior to that date.

After the splendidly consistent running achieved by the 'B12s' during the first 18 months of the new working, it has to be said that the early record of the 'B17s' must have presented a particularly dismal contrast, and the resumption of 'B12' working is likely to have provoked a certain amusement at Ipswich, where the latter were so well liked. In time the Ipswich crews came to appreciate the extra power which could be gained from the 'B17s' on the long trip to Manchester, but the class could hardly have been at the top of the popularity poll in 1930.

At Gorton the resumption of regular 'B17' running may be said to have begun on 21 July, when No 2801 *Holkham* arrived, fresh from the inevitable seven-month spell in Stratford Works. In a sense this was the real beginning of 'B17' working, for with new engines on order and shortly to be delivered, the class was never again to lose its hold on the 'Continental' for as long as lodging lasted. Noted working the down train on 23 August and 11 September, No 2801 held the fort alone until the end of October, when the brand-new No 2816 *Fallodon* arrived on the scene. Though fresh from overhaul and fitted with a new set of frames, No 2801 was evidently not considered quite up to the mark for the 'Continental' working, and it had been transferred back to the GE section by the end of the year. Its replacement by No 2816 hints at the importance attached to the Continental by the Loco Running Department, as this was the third time that a brand-new 'B17' had been sent to Gorton to operate the turn. It is possible also that the bad reputation earned by the original 'B17s' as a result of this early episode of the frames, clung on even after the repairs had been carried out, and it is interesting that none of the first 10 engines was ever again allocated to Gorton Loco.

As a contrast to the chopping and changing which had so far taken place at Gorton, the new arrival, No 2816, settled down to what was to prove a very lengthy spell, during which it became one of Gorton's most regular performers on a whole range of fast passenger turns up to 1938. It was soon to be joined by what was to become an equally well-known partner, No 2834 *Hinching-brooke*, and together these two put in thousands of miles on the Manchester-Ipswich road.

Unfortunately, notes covering the early days of this partnership are extremely sparse, and it is not until April 1932 that details become available which give us some insight into how the two engines were worked. By this time No 2834 had been at Gorton for about eight months and the pair were well settled on the 'Continental' working. In the week beginning Monday 4 April, No 2816 worked all three round trips to Ipswich, and did the same in the week following; then came the turn of No 2834, working to Ipswich on Monday 18 April and continuing for a total of three consecutive weeks without a break before giving way to No 2816 again on Monday 9 May. Other notes suggest that this somewhat irregular rostering pattern was the usual rule, rather than the more obvious system of using the two engines turn and turn about each week. The irregularities became even more noticeable of course when either of the pair was out of traffic for repairs, as occurred for instance during June and early July 1932, when No 2816 was in Stratford Works; during this period No 2834 continued to work the Gorton diagram single-handed, although there was one very fleeting appearance of a 'B12', No 8533, which arrived in Manchester Central on the down

train on 9 June and took out the up train the next day. No more appearances of this engine were recorded, and it was presumably used at short notice to cover for No 2834 during a temporary indisposition. During early 1933 the two faithful 'B17s' could still be seen in action, sometimes working weeks about, sometimes one of them operating the turn for as long as three weeks without a break.

At Ipswich the building of the new batch of 'B17s' soon had its effect, with No 2820 *Clumber* and No 2821 *Hatfield House* arriving there late in November 1930, and No 2825 *Raby Castle* the following February. All were to do a great deal of work on the 'Continental' during the next few years, although once again notes of their early work have been hard to come by, and the only ones known to be extant are of No 2820, which worked the up train out of Manchester on 7 and 30 March 1931. The latter day was a Monday – possibly a hint of a substitution at the Gorton end.

In the days of the 'B12s' it had been usual for the drivers and their engines to work alternate trips to Manchester, and this sytem continued into the 1930s, so that in any normal week it was usual to find a different engine working to Manchester in the middle than at the beginning, although with more than two engines now apparently rostered for the 'Continental' there was not the same regular sequence of alternate engines as had been noticed before. A good example can be seen in the same weeks of April and May already referred to in connection with Gorton engines. In the week beginning Monday 4 April No 2821 did the first round trip, and No 2825 the next two; the week after, No 2825 did the first trip and then gave way to No 2821 for the rest of the week; No 2821 went to Manchester again on the following Monday, and also on the Friday, with No 2820 working the mid-week trip. On Monday 25 April it was the turn of No 2820 to start off the week, and this engine then broke the usual sequence by doing the next two trips, probably because its partner No 2821 had been called upon to deputise for a failed Gorton engine early in the week, after having presumably been prepared for the Wednesday trip to Manchester. The latter was noted arriving in Manchester Central on the down train of Tuesday, presumably with Gorton men in charge, and duly worked back to Ipswich on the up train the following day. Gorton's No 2834 *Hinchingbrooke* appears to have been the culprit, and is presumed to have remained at Ipswich from its arrival on Monday evening to the return trip of Thursday, when it at last arrived safe and sound in Manchester.

The early 1930s saw some interesting changes in the crewing arrangements. At Gorton the regular fireman since the introduction of lodging had been

Jack Pomfret, whose partnership with Driver Howard went back even further; a typical GCR fireman, tall and powerfully built, he regarded himself with considerable justification as among the elite of Gorton men, having worked his way to the top in record time by a combination of enthusiasm and sheer strength of arm. His rapid advance proved his undoing however, for at the very time he was establishing himself on the 'Continental' there was growing pressure from the railway trade unions to bring in a system of job allocation by seniority. Complaints had not infrequently been voiced at Gorton when, either by favouritism or sheer good fortune, firemen succeeded in attaching themselves to senior drivers, thereby gaining a regular place on the mainline roster and enjoying greater financial rewards than colleagues who had entered the service years before them. Jack Pomfret was a case in point; although indisputably the best-remunerated fireman at Gorton Loco, he had started on the GCR only in 1919, and at the time he was on the 'Continental' there were men with longer service still working in the coal-train links. The general acceptance of promotion by seniority therefore signalled the end of his time as the regular 'Continental' fireman, and he duly bowed out in favour of a more senior man, Fred Crump; the latter's starting-date of December 1913 offers an instructive contrast with Pomfret's career, and indicates the extent to which the last-named had been promoted ahead of his time. The date of this change cannot be given with any certainty, but is thought to have come about during 1930. At round about the same time Driver Howard also relinquished the 'Continental', having been promoted Loco Inspector. His successor is believed to have been David Horne, who is remembered by several Ipswich men as having partnered Fireman Crump.

A more sweeping change took place about 1933, when the turn was incorporated into the Gorton Top Link. This was a logical step since the 'Continental' was a main-line lodging turn closely comparable with the London workings. In the senior link at this period were Drivers Jim Rangeley, Algy Roberts, Jimmy Rickards, Jack Glover and George Bourne, David Horne automatically becoming a member when the 'Continental' turn was included in the roster. Of the existing link, only Driver Rickards never worked the 'Continental'; he had expressed such a strong dislike of the 'B17s' that he refused point-blank to work them, and so when it came his turn to go to Ipswich as the weekly roster moved round, arrangements were made whereby he changed over with another crew.

The decision to bring the 'Continental' into the Top Link was no doubt welcomed by the men concerned, as they were now responsible for working four of the highly lucrative lodging jobs. Furthermore the Ipswich run was rather more of a 'soft touch' than the testing London turns, not only because of the easier schedules, but also the very convenient hours. Arriving at Ipswich late in the evening, the Gorton crews were on duty again at 6.30 the next morning, and they greatly appreciated this stop-over of not much more than nine hours. A further good point was the booking-off time of 1.50pm at Guide Bridge, giving the opportunity of a leisurely evening at home, or spent socially at the 'local' or the cinema – pleasures which footplatemen could never consider as taken for granted, in contrast to other occupations.

At Ipswich the crewing arrangements had been governed by the rule of seniority almost from the start. Directly Drivers Pack and Pinkney had been chosen to take charge of the working, a meeting of the local branch of ASLEF was held at which it was agreed that all future crews, both drivers and firemen, should be chosen strictly on seniority – no doubt the obvious financial rewards were a direct cause of this. Thus it came about that when the two firemen, Ernie Payne and Harry Church, moved on to new responsibilities during 1929, their places were taken by the next most senior men. Similarly, when Drivers Pinkney and Pack came off the working the jobs went to the next in line, in this instance Charlie Cross and Arthur Kemp. No precise dates can be given for the change of drivers, but there is no doubt that the disappearance of Pinkney and Pack from the scene was very much the end of an era. Both had started on the Great Eastern in the early 1890s, when the company was very much in its heyday, and they brought to the 'Continental' those high standards of efficiency, cleanliness and pride in the job which were so much a feature of the old pre-Grouping days. Jack Pack, for instance, was never quite satisfied with the efforts of the shed cleaners – he always insisted on shining up the buffers of his engine himself. When driving he seldom sat still, frequently making minute adjustments to the regulator, wiping the controls, polishing the fittings, or occasionally seizing the shovel from his mate to do a spell of firing. George Pinkney had a fetish about clean footplates after having once sustained a broken ankle as a result of treading on a stray piece of coal; this had given him a slight limp, and no matter how heavy the firing, the footplate of his engine had to be kept meticulously clean at all times. His original 'B12', No 8535, was known as 'The Pride of Ipswich', no doubt on account of its immaculate condition both inside and out. Probably both he and Jack Pack were sad to give up their 'B12s' for the new 'B17s', and it is a pity that there is no record of their reaction to the change; both had a considerable spell on 'B17s' before coming off the job, Pack in charge of No 2806 *Audley End* and Pinkney of No 2807 *Blickling*.

For Ipswich men the 'Continental' was not quite as attractive a job as at Gorton, particularly from the point of view of hours spent away from home. The early afternoon arrival at Guide Bridge meant a stay of almost 24 hours before they were off home again, and their return was too late for any social activity other than perhaps a few drinks in the local pub. No doubt it was for this reason that the system of alternating trips had been introduced. On certain occasions during the summer season it was possible for the crews to get home earlier by working a Saturday Only express to East Anglia which usually left Manchester Central at 9.13 in the morning; on this they were able to reach home by 3.30pm, no doubt a much appreciated facility on a Saturday afternoon. The train was seen by an observer at March on 12 August 1933 behind No 2821 *Hatfield House*, returning home after working the down 'Continental'. When the Ipswich engine was diagrammed in this way other arrangements had of course to be made for the 'Continental', a spare Gorton crew usually working it as far as Lincoln where it was handed over to the Great Eastern section; the engine and men then returned as required, often on one of the many relief or seasonal trains from the East Coast which operated on summer Saturdays. The arrangement was of course very popular with the Ipswich crews, but does not seem to have been continued after about 1934.

An important development occurred in the spring of 1933, when the decision was taken to re-equip the Gorton Top Link with 'B17' engines; this saw the arrival in Manchester of three brand-new members of the class, No 2840 *Somerleyton Hall*, No 2841 *Gayton Hall*, and No 2842 *Kilverstone Hall*, followed a little later by an older engine, No 2824 *Lumley Castle*, previously at Parkeston. Within a matter of days they were put to work on the London lodging turns,[5] and soon appeared on the 'Continental'; No 2841 *Gayton Hall* made its debut at the end of June, being noted on the up train on Friday the 30th. No 2842 *Kilverstone Hall* appeared on the scene on Monday 10 July, taking out the up train, and the earliest record of No 2840 *Somerleyton Hall* is Wednesday 30 August, again on the up train. These appearances suggest that the decision to incorporate the 'Continental' turn into the Top Link had been taken by this time. No 2824 *Lumley Castle* is recorded as having arrived at Gorton in the middle of November, and had its

first run to Ipswich with the up train on Monday 11 December, although this was an isolated out-and-back working and it was not seen again on the turn for some time; *Lumley Castle* was an engine with a poor reputation and it was not often used on the long-distance jobs.

The Gorton pattern of working at this period was for individual engines to work the 'Continental' a week at a time, with their regular drivers, although a nine-week sample of running in January and February 1934 shows some variations. thus: *Gayton Hall* was in charge during the first week (beginning Monday 8 January), then came *Kilverstone Hall* the next week; *Gayton Hall* again took over in the third week, but on the Friday/Saturday round trip was replaced by *Hinchingbrooke*, which then took the following week except again for the Friday and Saturday when *Lumley Castle* did another of its odd trips; in the fifth week came *Kilverstone Hall*, then *Hinchingbrooke*, *Kilverstone Hall* again, *Gayton Hall*, and finally *Hinchingbrooke* again. It is a pity that there is no information as to who the drivers were during these weeks. Of the absentee engines, No 2816 *Fallodon* was due to go into Stratford Works for overhaul, while No 2840 *Somerleyton Hall* did an odd week (beginning 12 March), but for some reason does not seem to have been used as much as the other 'B17s' at this time. Perhaps the most surprising event of the summer was the four consecutive weeks of work put in by none other than *Lumley Castle*, a most unusual development; beginning on Monday 6 August, it never missed a single trip between then and Saturday 1 September, when it duly arrived in Manchester Central with the down train. The use of the same engine for such a long period was very rare on the Gorton lodging turns.

It was during this same August that the alternative working described earlier was again in operation, with the Ipswich engine seen leaving Central on several consecutive Saturday mornings; in its place, the up 'Continental' was taken out on 11 August by No 5427 *City of London*, and on 18 August by No 2834 *Hinchingbrooke*, these engines probably working as far as Lincoln. On 25 August the train was worked, most unusually, by a Woodford 'B7', No 5038, which may have come off at Sheffield if it was being worked back to its home shed. In each of these cases Gorton crews are likely to have been in charge, and it was of course on busy days such as these that the up-and-coming young footplatemen sometimes had the unexpected opportunity of working an important mainline turn, with most of the regular men either off duty or out on the road.

During 1935 the number of 'B17s' at Gorton was reduced to three because of engines moving to Neasden, and this trio, Nos 2816, 2840 and 2841 ept the 'Continental' service running from late January until the end of the year, when the London-based engines were transferred back again. With them came a new arrival on the scene, No 2830 *Thoresby Park*, better known by its later name of *Tottenham Hotspur*. By this period Gorton Works was carrying out major overhauls to the 'B17' class, the work having been transferred from Stratford, and No 2830 completed its repairs on 7 December; having been run-in in the usual way it remained at the Loco and took its place in the Top Link. It made its first trip to Ipswich on Monday 30 December.

The Ipswich workings continued to follow the pattern already described, although it was noticeable that greater reliance was placed on the newer engines of the class. No 2806 *Audley End* was not noted at all between Tuesday 28 March 1933 and Tuesday 2 January 1934, both these being up workings. An even longer gap occurred between Friday 29 June 1934, when it deputised for Gorton's *Hinchingbrooke* on the up train, and August 1935. During these spells of absence it made no fewer than four visits to Stratford Works for repairs of one sort or another, all of which kept it out of traffic for a total of four months. No 2807 *Blickling* was similarly absent from the 'Continental' workings between February 1933 and February 1934. The brunt of the work was thus carried by Nos 2820, 2821 and 2825, although No 2801 *Holkham* took a share of things in the spring of 1935. Officially allocated to Parkeston, *Holkham* came on the scene on 24 April, when it worked to Manchester; it was probably on loan to cover the absence of No 2821, which had gone into Stratford for repairs a few days previously. Soon afterwards No 2820 also went in for repair, and *Holkham* remained until at least 28 June, when it was noted on the down train.

A typical week's working of early 1935 therefore looked like this:

	Up	Down
Monday	2840	2821
Tuesday	2821	2840
Wednesday	2840	2825
Thursday	2825	2840
Friday	2840	2821
Saturday	2821	2840

The engines involved were Nos 2821 *Hatfield House* and 2825 *Raby Castle* of Ipswich, and No 2840 *Somerleyton Hall* of Gorton; the workings were for the week beginning 18 March 1935.

Engine failures on the 'Continental' were very infrequent, no doubt because of the high standards of maintenance at both sheds. Of the two places, Ipswich had slightly the better record, probably because of the somewhat easier work which its

engines did when not working to Manchester; at Gorton the Top Link engines had to work three lodging jobs to London as well as covering the Ipswich turn, and the practice of diagramming engines to work on the same job for a full week undoubtedly added to the burden. An interesting example occurred in the very first week of 1934 when after the Gorton engine (unidentified) had failed at Ipswich its place was taken by No 2820 *Clumber*, which then worked the rest of the week opposite its stablemate No 2806 *Audley End*. Such changes did not of course make any difference to the manning arrangements, but the Gorton men would naturally be a little apprehensive until they had got the full measure of their strange steed. One of Ipswich's rare failures occurred early in February 1935 when 'B4' No 6104 of March Loco was seen in Manchester, and worked out of Central with the up train on Thursday the 7th, after having arrived with the corresponding train the previous afternoon. At this period the 'B4' engines were rare in Manchester except when they came to Gorton for repairs.

A change of locomotives took place at Ipswich in the spring of 1935, with No 2821 *Hatfield House* being replaced by a brand-new member of the 'B17' class, No 2845. On Saturday 22 June the new arrival was to be seen in Ipswich's Showground station, highly polished and much decorated for its ceremonial naming, which was performed by Major-General Sir John Ponsonby in the presence of a number of LNER dignitaries, including the Chairman William Whitelaw and Mr Nigel Gresley. Having been christened *The Suffolk Regiment*, No 2845 duly took its place in the Ipswich passenger roster, making the first of many trips to Manchester on Wednesday 3 July. It brought a touch of distinction to the service with its highly polished regimental badges on the splasher below each nameplate, although observers in the northwest would not have been slow to point out that the idea was copied from the LMS, whose 'Royal Scot' engines were a common sight in Manchester. No 2845 was to be a frequent performer on the 'Continental' right up to the war.

The most important event in the history of the 'Continental' during 1936, without any doubt, was the arrival of a batch of new 'B17' 'Footballers' at Gorton in the late spring. Much had been heard of these engines on the Great Central section for some time before they actually appeared, and there were rumours that they were to be something of an improvement on the original 'B17' series, but in the event the alleged 'new' type turned out to be nothing more than a basic 'B17' attached to an LNER standard tender instead of the GER type found on the earlier engines. As far as the 'Continental' was concerned, the main advantage which this conferred was that the crews were at last free of worry about running short of coal en route. Even in the days of the 'B12s' they had to guard constantly against waste of fuel, for the GER-type tender held only four tons, which over the distance of 215 miles between Manchester and Ipswich worked out at not much over 40lb/mile. So delicately balanced was the consumption, indeed, that when Driver Jack Howard once boasted that he was able to do the through trip on an average of 39lb per mile, his opposite number George Pinkney refused to believe it, claiming that this 'consumption figure' was the result of a private arrangement between Driver Howard and the coal-stage hands by which additional unrecorded amounts of coal were placed on the tender in exchange for a tip. Whether this story is true or not, Jack Howard's alleged claim cannot have been that much of an exaggeration in view of the figures quoted above.

The introduction of 'B17' engines made the situation worse rather than better, for although a considerably bigger locomotive than the 'B12s', they had exactly the same size tender, thus requiring even more careful management on the footplate. The difficulty was overcome as far as possible by what was known at Gorton as 'cobbing up' – making a wall of large lumps round the tender so as to stack extra coal on top – and by this means it was possible to exceed the official capacity quite considerably. However, this could not easily be done at places where an automatic coaling plant was in use, as at Gorton from 1933. Some attempt was made to provide higher coal guards, though this was allegedly done to prevent the fire-irons becoming jammed by spillage into the tender sides[6]. The difficulties were not really solved until the introduction of the standard tenders on the 'Footballers', which held twice as much as the originals.

The small GER-type tender had been a necessary fitting because of the restrictions on engine length which existed on the Great Eastern section, but by 1936 these had been considerably eased and the 'Footballers' were able to work on the 'Continental' from the very start. The first to come to Gorton were Nos 2859 *Norwich City*, 2860 *Hull City* and 2861 *Sheffield Wednesday*, looking very different from the earlier engines not only with their much bigger tenders but also with the representation of a football on the splasher below each nameplate, flanked by panels displaying the club colours. As is well known, No 2859 was later rebuilt in streamlined form and given a different name, but it operated from Gorton for well over a year in its original condition. It was the first of the new trio to appear on the 'Continental', working

the turn for two consecutive weeks from Monday 6 July. It was followed immediately by No 2861 *Sheffield Wednesday*, which worked the full week up to and including Saturday 25 July. No 2834 *Hinchingbrooke* was in charge the following week, and then came the debut of No 2860 *Hull City*, which worked the first week of August.

The work of these three engines was soon interrupted by the need for repairs, and during October and November they were all stopped for this purpose, being sent most unusually to Darlington for attention; this hints at something of a special nature, but the reason remains a mystery. During this period No 2861 notched up the first failure of these engines on the 'Continental'; having worked to Ipswich on Wednesday 2 September it failed to arrive on the next day's return, being replaced en route by old favourite No 2821 *Hatfield House*, now allocated to March. The reason for its disappearance was probably quite serious as No 2821 continued to deputise for it right into the following week and did not return to its parent shed until at least the middle of the month. No 2861 made no more appearances on the 'Continental' that year, and after the end of September spent most of the time in Darlington Works. The other two 'Footballers' struggled on into 1937, doing odd stints on the 'Continental' but obviously not making a very big impact because of visits to Darlington and their use on other diagrams. No 2859 failed to return from Ipswich on Thursday 8 October and was replaced by another old-timer of the 'Continental' workings, No 2806 *Audley End*; it went to Darlington shortly after and was not seen again on the 'Continental' for over a month. No 2860 is known to have done a week-long stint from 14 September but was seldom seen at Ipswich after that, perhaps being utilised more frequently on the London turns.

The impact of the 'Footballers' became much more noticeable from February 1937, when a further series began to come into service. Four of these were allocated to Gorton, beginning with the first, No 2862 *Manchester United*; its trip to Ipswich on Monday 15 February was its first in regular service. No 2869 *Barnsley* was the next to be added to Gorton's allocation, and made its 'Continental' debut on Monday 21 June. No 2871 *Manchester City* followed on 12 July and No 2872 *West Ham United* on 13 September, both of these dates being Mondays.

At the time the 'Footballers' were coming into service the quest for more intensive utilisation of locomotives was at its height. This was part of the general economy drive which had formed a major part of LNER policy since the adverse financial trends of the previous decade, and which had grown in intensity until it reached into every sphere of the company's operations. In the locomotive department, longer diagrams were the order of the day as the management sought to extract the maximum productive mileage from each unit. Thus it was that on Monday 30 November 1936 a new and much extended diagram came into operation whereby instead of retiring to Gorton Loco after arriving from Ipswich, the engine of the 'Continental' was scheduled to work an evening train to Leicester, returning to Manchester in the early hours of the morning on the down Mail from Marylebone. This increased the daily aggregate mileage to almost double the previous figure – 215 to over 400, not counting light engine running and short trips between Manchester Central and Guide Bridge; workings such as this were becoming increasingly common in the late 1930s, as was the practice of remanning – the engine passed through the hands of three different sets of men between leaving Ipswich and arriving at its berth on Gorton Loco. In earlier years remanning had been almost unknown on main-line passenger workings over the Great Central.

To work this much larger diagram the engine of the down 'Continental' proceeded direct to Trafford Park Loco after reaching Manchester, in order to take on coal; it then worked a trip to Guide Bridge and back on local trains, arriving back in Central at 5.59pm, and after a wait for over an hour during which the station turntable was made use of, the engine left on the 7.22pm Manchester-Leicester train. All remanning took place at Guide Bridge, a set of reliefmen taking over the incoming 'Continental' and then giving way to a Gorton No 2 Link crew on the 7.22pm. The new diagram did not operate on Saturdays; instead the engine of the 'Continental' worked back to Guide Bridge on the 4.28pm stopping train from Central and then proceeded as it had done in former times direct to Gorton. To work the 7.22pm from Central an engine left Gorton at 6.25pm, running light to the terminus as the rather more sparse Saturday evening service did not offer a train which it could conveniently work from Guide Bridge. The first engine definitely known to have worked the full diagram was Gorton's No 2840 *Somerleyton Hall* on Tuesday 8 December 1936, and the first Ipswich engine recorded was No 2845 *The Suffolk Regiment* on 21 December. A stand-by engine was always on hand in case of difficulties after the arrival of the 'Continental'; the latter working naturally took precedence over the 7.22pm, and if the incoming engine had developed a fault it was sent direct to Gorton to be got ready for the next day's working to Ipswich. This happened, for example, on Monday 26 April 1937, when No 2845 *The Suffolk Regiment* was replaced on the Leicester working by No 5501 *Mons*; the 'B17' went to Gorton after arrival and

duly went back on the 'Continental' the following day.

During the final two years or so before the service was suspended on the outbreak of war there were further changes in the locomotive situation. The trend at Gorton was for the original 'B17s' to move away as the 'Footballers' assumed command, although the process was a gradual one and No 2834 *Hinchingbrooke* actually lingered until early in 1939. For the last 18 months however it can be safely said that the Gorton half of the 'Continental' was completely dominated by the 'Footballers', even though these were not quite the same ones as at the time of the original allocation; Nos 2859 and 2861 had left during 1937 and were replaced early in the following year by Nos 2864 *Liverpool* and 2865 *Leicester City*, though neither of these did much work on the 'Continental' and No 2865 was transferred away again during the summer. This engine did an odd trip on the 18 July, only a matter of days before it was moved. During 1939 more of the 'Footballers' were sent away as larger engines began to take over Gorton's passenger workings[7] and by the early summer the allocation had shrunk to two. An irony of this situation was that several of the 'Footballers' were sent to Ipswich as a result of a further relaxation of restrictions on the GE section, and they thus began to appear on the 'Continental' from the southern end as well as from Gorton, for example on Saturday 10 June, when No 2857 *Doncaster Rovers* took the up train out of Manchester. However, the original 'B17s' were never swamped as they had been at Gorton; No 2805 *Lincolnshire Regiment* had arrived in May 1938 after an overhaul at Gorton and was noted on the down 'Continental' on Wednesday the 25th, remaining very much in the forefront of things during the next 12 months; it replaced one of the old stagers of the Ipswich-Manchester runs, No 2807 *Blickling*, which moved away after putting in nearly 10 years of continuous service at Ipswich, apart from a short spell at Parkeston. *Blickling* was far from being on its own in achieving such a long spell of service, for Nos 2806, 2820 and 2825 were still going strong in 1939, none of them ever having left Ipswich from the time they were first allocated there.

By 1939 there were a number of changes among the driving personnel. The Gorton Top Link now consisted of George Bourne, Jack Glover, Jack Garston, Tommy Evans and Jim Fielding; presumably there were now only five drivers instead of six as formerly because of the reduction in London lodging jobs which had come about in 1937. At Ipswich Charlie Cross had come off the job, and Arthur Kemp was now in partnership with Ernie Gould. With the exception of Jim Fielding, who died suddenly during August, these men were in charge when the 'Continental' was suspended in September.

The story of the York portion of the 'Continental' is something quite separate, at any rate as far as its more northerly routing is concerned. As a result of changes made just a few weeks before Grouping the York coaches had been timetabled to travel via Sheffield, being detached from the main train on arrival there and worked forward to York at 2pm on the Oxford-Glasgow through train; they returned by the same route, rejoining the main train at Sheffield Victoria. In the down direction however this arrangement was very soon modified, with the coaches being rescheduled to come off at Sleaford, whence they were worked forward via Ancaster and Barkston to connect with an East Coast main line express at Grantham. Passengers going in this direction thus avoided all contact with the GC system, although coming south they still travelled via Sheffield as before. The coaches were conveyed from York on the Glasgow-Southampton train reaching Sheffield Victoria at 4.12pm, and here they were detached to await the arrival of the main train. Between York and Sheffield the Southampton train was worked by the North Eastern area, and passengers thus travelled behind engines from three difference sections of the LNER between York and Harwich. At Sheffield Victoria there was of course a considerable delay, not only to attach the York coaches, but also because the main train had usually to be split to allow the engine and leading coaches to proceed beyond Sheffield as the Manchester-Cleethorpes express, an arrangement mentioned earlier in this chapter. During this period therefore the 'Continental' was allowed a wait of 13 minutes at Sheffield Victoria, and another feature of the arrangements was that the York coaches were diagrammed to work through to Glasgow and back, being advertised thus in the public timetables.

All these things came to an end in 1927, on the same date as the Gorton-Ipswich lodging turn was introduced. Under a complete restructuring of the timetable the York portion was now diagrammed to attach and detach at Lincoln, and was worked in both directions by engines from Lincoln Loco. The schedule had thus reverted to something approaching its original form[8], in the days when the GER had worked through trains from Liverpool Street to York via what they called the 'Cathedrals Route'. So far as locomotive working was concerned, however, the situation of 1927 was a good deal different from that of pre-Grouping days, chiefly because of a decline in Great Eastern influence at Lincoln. A rationalisation programme put in hand by the LNER saw the closure of the former GER locomotive shed about 1925, and the transfer of its engines and men to the former GCR and GNR sheds, which had the advantage of being much nearer the station and yards. Here composite links were formed in which men from all three pre-Grouping companies worked side by side, learning former GCR, GNR and GER roads indiscriminately. The GER shed was retained as a servicing point, no doubt because of its proximity to the yard at Pyewipe, but without any resident staff the facilities were restricted to turning and watering.

Passenger workings were mainly concentrated at the former GCR shed, where they came under the control of a Depot Superintendent who believed strongly in the virtues of Great Central locomotives. This was Toby Morris, a former GCR man who had previously been in charge at Keadby Loco; under his regime at Lincoln increasingly wide use was made of Great Central engines on passenger turns, and in these things can be detected, yet again, the hand of that eminence grise of the LNER Southern Area, W. G. P. Maclure.

Despite its outward resemblance to the former GER working therefore, the new Lincoln-York turn was primarily a GCR affair, as the evidence of the first day's working clearly shows. In charge of the York portion of the 'Continental' on that first Saturday, 14 May 1927, was 'D9' No 5113, generally regarded at this period as the 'top engine' at Lincoln Loco, and it is understood that the all-GCR crew were Driver George Dean and Fireman George Moore. The former was a well-known character in Lincoln and district, and in the course of an interesting career he had been involved in the serious Brocklesby accident of 1907 while working a Grimsby-Lincoln fish train. George Moore was his regular fireman at this period, and the two made many trips together on the York working. Departure from Lincoln was originally at 11.35am for an arrival in York at 1.10pm, the return trip bringing the train back into Lincoln in time to connect with the main arrival from Liverpool and Manchester at 5.20pm. The diagram was thus a straight out-and-back trip to York, with virtually the same starting and finishing times as the former Sheffield working on the main train, and so the new turn slotted in neatly to replace the old.

During 1928 there came a somewhat unexpected reminder of former practices with the arrival at Lincoln of some ex-GER 'Claud Hamilton' engines. Nos 8829 and 8868 came on the scene in the spring, and were eventually followed the year after by Nos 8808 and 8874, with No 8868 departing again a little later[9]. The reason for these developments, almost certainly, was to do with the problems of working Westinghouse-braked coaching stock, for which the 'D9' engines were not fitted. Although the sets of coaches for the 'Continental' were dual-braked, ie: carried both Westinghouse and vacuum brakes, it often happened that strengthening vehicles had to be provided at Harwich, and at that period the only ones available were of GER origin, complete with the Westinghouse brakes which had been standard on that railway. Thus a famous GER class came back to Lincoln after an absence of a number of years, and it is interesting to wonder about the sort of reception they received from the Great Central men; probably it was a favourable one, because they were in many ways a closely comparable type to the GCR 'D9', and had the characteristic GER sturdiness already mentioned in connection with Class B12 engines.

In the event their stay on the York working was not a very long one. The gradual introduction of LNER-designed stock on various main-line services brought about a down-grading of vacuum-fitted vehicles, which thus became available for second-line duties such as strengthening, and so the need for the 'Clauds' at Lincoln began to disappear. They finally departed from the scene about the end of 1931, by which time the solitary Lincoln 'D9', No 5113, had been joined by sister engine No 6034, and the two were putting in some regular work on the York 'Continental'. Very few notes appear to have survived from these years, and the only definite sighting of a 'Claud' that can be quoted on the 'Continental' is Saturday 21 June 1930, when No 8808 was noted at York; no doubt this was a day when the normal train had been strengthened, hence the need to make use of one of the 'Clauds'. 'D9s' are more likely to have been in evidence on weekdays, for example on Wednesday 30 January 1929, when the faithful No 5113 arrived at York.

Another type which Lincoln sometimes used on the turn were the 'B5' 4-6-0s, which although widely known as the 'Fish' engines were a popular choice for passenger work, no doubt because of the influence of Toby Morris. No 6067 was seen at York on Wednesday 7 November 1928, probably used in preference to the 'Clauds' as it had recently been rebuilt with a raised boiler which incorporated a superheater.

By 1930 the York diagram had been expanded to work the engine through two shifts. The first crew came off the shed at 7.10 in the morning and worked the 7.30 Lincoln-Grantham train, getting back to Lincoln at 10.31; a second set of men came on duty at 11 o'clock at the shed and walked to the station to take charge, the engine standing prepared to take over the through working to Manchester in the event of a failure of the regular Gorton or Ipswich engine. Because of the

admirable consistency of the main-line engines however there are no known instances of the substitution ever having taken place.

An important development of 1935 was the arrival of the first six-coupled express passenger engines at Lincoln, these being a trio of the well-known 'Imminghams', Nos 6095, 6103 and 6104 recently displaced at March Loco by 'B17s'. The three newcomers arrived between July and October, and soon saw service on the York turn, although no dates have been traced. Generally considered very handsome engines, they must have created something of a stir at Lincoln by the fact that they were painted in the striking LNER green, unlike the 'D9s' which were now black. By this date No 6104 had exchanged the rather plain 'flowerpot' type of chimney for the curved style reminiscent of the original Robinson version, as possibly had the other two, and so in the eyes of many observers these new arrivals must have been a very welcome addition to the scenery.

At about the same time came an alteration to the manning arrangements whereby the original two-crew system gave way to full link working, the job being rotated between about half a dozen sets of men. This was a trend which was evident all over the LNER during these years, and may have owed something to union pressure. By 1936 the York job was being worked by a Top Link which included Drivers Phil Markham, Bob Salter and Bill Woods. Thus the days when the 'Continental' workings had been dominated for so long by individual drivers, such as Ralph Thompson and George Dean, were finally over, although even before the introduction of link working the original Great Central influence had been to some extent diluted by the inclusion in the roster of ex-GER men such as Jack Wheat and Walter Balaam.

As the newly formed link was settling down to work, further changes took place in the locomotive sphere. In the spring of 1936 a group of Class C4 Atlantics displaced from the GCR main line were sent to Lincoln, followed by a still more exciting arrival in the autumn, that of 'City' class No 5424 *City of Lincoln*. The earliest note that has been traced of this engine working to York is Friday 30 October, with Driver Salter and Fireman George Moore. Of the Atlantics, No 6089 was recorded on 7 and 8 January 1937 with Driver Phil Markham and Fireman H. Rossington, followed by No 5424 the next day with the same crew. A curiosity of the link working was that the men did not normally complete a full week of six trips on the York turn, but instead did the first three days and then switched over to a March job, changing with a set of men who had worked to March in the first half of the week. Drivers had to know two routes to York, as the 'Continental' worked northwards via the Knottingley line and returned along the main line through Selby; this arrangement had been introduced in 1935-36, allegedly to keep the line clear for the down 'Flying Scotsman', which was accelerated at this time[10].

Some effort appears to have been made to roster No 5424 *City of Lincoln* for the York job, although both Atlantics and 'Imminghams' appeared with some frequency. In December 1937 and the succeeding January No 5424 was in Gorton Works for repairs, and the other types shared the work during its absence. On Monday 10 January for instance, 'C4' No 6087 was in charge, followed by 'B4' No 6103 for the next two days.

City of Lincoln was eventually joined by a sister engine, No 5427, in June 1939, and the earliest note of its use on the 'Continental' is Monday 10 July. No 5424 was in charge the next day, and then No 5427 again. The pair were also noted in the week beginning Monday 21 August, and were probably sharing the job regularly at this time, although 'C4' No 5192 appeared on Saturday 26 August. By this time No 5427 was of course running without its *City of London* name, which had been removed in the autumn of 1937.

The 'Continental' is well remembered at Lincoln not only by the railway staff but also, in a less complimentary way, by the local inhabitants, on account of the very considerable interruption to road traffic which, from 1927 onwards, was caused by the lengthy manoeuvring process necessary to divide and join up the train. The shunting movements which these operations involved meant that the crossing gates at each end of the station had to be repeatedly closed, the worst interruption being caused by the up train as the first portion was due to arrive at 5.15pm, just as the evening rush was getting under way. This train ran through the station and on to the crossing, where it halted whilst the station shunters fixed clamps to the points behind it, and then reversed into No 2 platform, which was a bay. Whilst this was taking place the main train arrived and drew in at the up through platform, No 5, with the engine adjacent to the second of the two water-columns; after a quick top-up of the tank it was unhooked to draw forward and reverse onto the coaches waiting in Platform 2, which were then pulled out and propelled back onto the main train. The whole procedure was sandwiched into a very swift 17 minutes from the arrival of the York portion, but, with no fewer than four separate occupations of the busy Pelham Street crossing, the patience of road-users must have been considerably tried, especially when the process culminated in a fifth closing of the gates as the now much longer train finally ground its way across on the next stage of its journey.

Similar shunting occurred on the arrival of the down train, though the pattern of these movements varied over the years as the York portion was initially booked to leave after the main train, and then later was altered to precede it. The passage of the up and down 'Continentals' thus created a considerable amount of work for the Lincoln station staff, in addition to the routine tasks of attending to passengers and luggage.

The working of the 'Continental' over the Cheshire Lines remained unaffected by the changes of 1927, since reversal of the train in Manchester Central automatically meant a change of engine there. The CLC was always something of a contrast to the GC section proper, and may be fairly accurately described as a sort of separate world largely dominated by a limited number of engine classes. From about the mid-1920s express passenger workings were mainly the domain of the Class D6 4-4-0s, known to one and all as 'Pollitts', and it was machines of this type which, as described earlier, were responsible for working the 'Continental' between Manchester and Liverpool for a good number of years.

Nevertheless there are certain changes to be put on record. In the spring of 1929 a reorganisation of engine workings took place at Neepsend Loco, Sheffield, bringing into operation a number of turns to Liverpool and back, running via Manchester Central or Stockport Tiviot Dale at different times of the day. Diagrams of this sort had existed before the reorganisation, but included in the new workings was a homeward trip involving the up 'Continental', after an arrival in Liverpool at 12.27 on an express from Hull. These Sheffield workings were handled mainly by Class C1 Atlantics, and despite their Great Northern ancestry these engines had proved exceptionally popular at Neepsend since being introduced there soon after Grouping. Under the new arrangements the 'Continental' thus became a regular Atlantic turn between Liverpool and Manchester. Neepsend had particular members of Class C1 on its allocation for a long time, principally Nos 3287, 4412, 4420, 4428, 4434 and 4449. For the 'Continental' turn Neepsend appear to have made an effort to roster the same engine throughout the working week, though in practice it was not all that often that this was actually achieved; No 4420 worked the complete week beginning 6 November 1933, and in the following year the weeks beginning 8 January and 18 June were worked by Nos 4428 and 4442 respectively. More often the week was shared by two engines, as for instance from Monday 1 April 1935 when No 4412 did the first and last days of the week and No 4434 the rest; such patterns suggest that the drivers worked throughout the week, but not always with the same engines. Sometimes there was an even more varied mixture, such as from Monday 24 September 1934 when the first three days were worked by Nos 4428, 4420 and 3273 in sequence, followed by No 3287 for the rest of the week.

During 1933-35 Neepsend received a small allocation of Class D11 'Directors' previously at Gorton, and these also appeared on the 'Continental' turn; the earliest known workings are in the week beginning 11 September 1933, when No 5509 *Prince Albert* worked through from Monday to Friday inclusive. The following weeks saw more 'Directors' appearing on the scene – No 5501 *Mons* on Tuesday 26 September, and No 5511 *Marne* on the Thursday and Friday of the following week after No 5509 had done the previous two days. During these weeks there were also isolated appearances of Class D10 engines, Nos 5431 *Edwin A. Beazley* and 5435 *Sir Clement Royds*; both these had been based at Neepsend for some time, and their sudden emergence on the 'Continental' turn alongside the 'D11s' suggests that a positive effort was being made to roster 'Directors' regularly for the job, particularly on the evidence of weeks such as the following in 1933.

18 September No 5435 *Sir Clement Royds*
19 September No 5509 *Prince Albert*
20 September No 5509 *Prince Albert*
21 September No 5431 *Edwin A. Beazley*
22 September No 5509 *Prince Albert*
23 September no record

In fact, the 'Directors' disappeared quite abruptly from the scene early in the succeeding November and the 'C1' Atlantics came back in force. It has been suggested that the greater length of the 'Directors', though only a foot more than the Atlantics, created difficulties on the turntable at Manchester Central, and the fact that this turntable was extended in 1936 seems to lend some colour to this notion.

In the down direction the faithful 'Pollitts' continued to appear on the 'Continental' until well into the 1930s, presenting an interesting contrast in size and appearance to the 'B17' at the other end of the train when they backed on at Manchester Central. By 1930 the turn had become a Liverpool responsibility, and it was at Brunswick Loco that most of the 'D6s' were concentrated at this time, though their numbers at both ends of the route were soon to be thinned by withdrawals. Unfortunately no specific sightings of 'D6s' on the down 'Continental' have been traced.

The Liverpool turn disappeared from the rosters in late November 1936, when the workings were completely revolutionised by the introduction of a new set of diagrams operated from Gorton, involving several trips to Liverpool and for which a special link had to be formed. The aim behind this was to achieve more intensive engine utilisation, and the new diagrams involved long mileages; the Gorton engine which now appeared at the head of the down 'Continental' had begun its day at 1.20am, and got as far afield as Nottingham before eventually arriving light in Manchester Central about an hour before the down train was due.

An equal novelty was the type of engine used. For some time prior to the introduction of this working Gorton had been making increasing use of Class K3 engines on secondary passenger jobs, and by the close of 1936 had no fewer than 12 of them on its allocation; despite their smaller driving wheels and well-known tendency to ride roughly, they appear to have acquired a good name among the GCR footplate staff as passenger engines. Thus the down 'Continental' became a regular 'K3' working from the first day that the new diagrams were introduced, which was Monday 30 November 1936, and the engine on that occasion was No 2466. Between January and March 1937 Gorton acquired a batch of new 'K3s' which had been run-in at Doncaster, and all of these eventually made their appearance on the Continental. The first to do so was No 3816 on Monday 1 February, followed by No 3814 on Saturday 20 February.

For a short time during July and August 1937 the turn was switched to 'B17' engines, No 2860 *Hull City* being the most frequent performer, but in the autumn the 'K3s' took over again, with No 3814 starting off the new sequence on Saturday 4 September after No 2834 *Hinchingbrooke* had worked to Liverpool the previous day. It was during this second phase of 'K3' working that an accident occurred, the only serious one to befall the 'Continental' during LNER days. On Monday 4 October, No 3817 was working the train, with Driver Frank Duckworth and Fireman Wilf Ellison on the footplate after taking over from the early turn crew at Guide Bridge in the usual way; as they approached Liverpool Central Driver Duckworth misjudged his whereabouts while passing through the tunnels – a notoriously tricky section – and so entered the station precincts at too high a speed. Heeling over on the sharp left-hand curve into No 1 platform, the 'K3' came into violent contact with the stonework, its cylinder cover ploughing up the copings and throwing out a shower of stones and debris. Fortunately the engine stayed on the rails and the train was brought to a halt without any injuries being caused, although the force of the impact had thrown Driver Duckworth on to the footplate floor.

With the outbreak of war and suspension of Continental steamer services at the beginning of September 1939, the 'North Country Continental' was withdrawn from the timetables. Not until long after the end of the war was it to be restored, and by that time many things had changed, not least in the locomotive sphere where lodging turns had long since been abandoned and were never to be restored; the long through workings of the interwar years thus passed into history, and with them something of the fascination of the 'Continental'.

To add to the notes and recollections recorded in this chapter, a few anecdotes from the interwar years may be mentioned. There was the time, for instance, when the train was brought to a sudden halt at Pinchbeck, on the GN&GE Joint Line, when the communication cord was pulled. The staff discovered that the person responsible was a Catholic priest who had unfortunately become locked in the lavatory; they duly released him, and to save his blushes reset the valve without revealing his identity.

A rather more dramatic incident occurred at Mottram and Broadbottom on Tuesday 22 September 1936; local residents were surprised that afternoon when instead of racing through the station as usual on its way up to Woodhead, the up train came to a halt at the platform. The reason, though they were not to know at the time, was that the train staff were in pursuit of a passenger who had suddenly lost his reason and was running up and down the corridors without clothes on; directly the train stopped he jumped out and ran about the station buildings, eventually seizing a long mop and poking with it at the wheels of the engine (No 2806 *Audley End*), watched by an interested Ipswich crew. Eventually he was cornered and the train proceeded. Testimony of its usual punctuality was given by Mr Harry Norman, landlord of the nearby Griffin Inn, who afterwards remarked to a newspaper reporter that he was in the habit of setting his clock by the passing of the up express every afternoon.

An occurrence of a sporting nature took place in the early days of the through working when Jack Pomfret, the first Gorton fireman to work to Ipswich, had occasion to go to the signalbox after the train had been halted at Chippenham Junction, not far from Newmarket; arriving in the box he was most surprised to find the signalman taking not the slightest notice either of him or the train, but looking in the opposite direction through a pair of binoculars; it transpired that he was watching a racehorse being exercised, and he strongly advised Fireman Pomfret to place a bet on it when it ran a few days later in the Cambridgeshire Stakes. The fireman and his driver, Jack Howard, duly took note of this, and their faith in the signalman was suitably rewarded when *Double Life* came in as winner of the 1929 Cambridgeshire at 20 to 1. The identity of the turf expert has never been revealed, and whether any other railway crews ever obtained racing information at Chippenham Junction is not known, though this incident suggests they would have been well advised to do so.

Many other tales could be told – such as the occasion when for some inexplicable reason the up train was stopped by signals at Hadfield West and was unable to restart until the Old Dinting pilot had been fetched to give it a push, nearly causing a stand-up fight between the driver of the 'Continental' and the signalman – but it is time to close this account with a final glimpse at the locomotive side of the story. Strangest appearance of all in the last few weeks before the outbreak of war was that of Gorton 'Green Arrow' No 4828 at Lincoln, working the up train on Wednesday 14 June; presumably it did not continue beyond March as such heavy engines were of course barred on the GE section. The story behind this is not known, but the occurrence hints at a revision of the arrangements on the GCR part of the route, for this was a time when more and more Great Central expresses were being worked by larger locomotives, as we have told elsewhere[11]. However, this must remain in the realm of speculation, and as far as is known no plans of this kind ever came to fruition either before or after World War 2.

Notes

1   C. J. Allen, *Titled Trains of Great Britain*.
2   Railway Correspondence & Travel Society, *Locomotives of the LNER, Part 2B*.
3   See Chapter 7.
4   Railway Correspondence & Travel Society, *Locomotives of the LNER, Part 2B*, p101.
5   D. Jackson & O. Russell, *The Great Central in LNER Days*, Chapter 4.
6   Railway Correspondence & Travel Society, *Locomotives of the LNER, Part 2B*, p108.
7   D. Jackson & O. Russell, *The Great Central in LNER Days*, Chapter 6.
8   C. J. Allen, *Titled Trains of Great Britain*.
9   Railway Correspondence & Travel Society, *Locomotives of the LNER, Part 3C*, p46.
10 C. J. Allen, *Titled Trains of Great Britain*.
11 Jackson & Russell, *The Great Central in LNER Days*, Chapter 6.

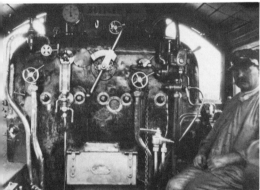

Above:
Chorlton Junction, Manchester, in 1928. 'B12' No 8535 of Ipswich heads the up 'North Country Continental' with Driver George Pinkney and Fireman Ernie Payne on the footplate. *W. Potter collection*

Left:
'Pride of Ipswich'. This was the nickname given to 'B12' No 8535, and here Driver George Pinkney is seen in the cab. *E. A. Payne*

Below:
A 'B12' at Gorton. Photographed close to the Gorton coaling hopper, No 8520 is believed to have arrived on a special working in the summer of 1933.
Photo H. N. James

Top left:
The 'Pollitts' did a great deal of work on the 'North Country Continental' between Manchester and Liverpool. Here is No 5880 at Trafford Park Loco at some date in the 1930s. *Photomatic*

Centre left:
Besides working the 'Continental' west of Lincoln, the 'D9s' were common at Sheffield on a variety of passenger jobs. No 6021 *Queen Mary* is seen at the east end of the station on 14 September 1929.
Photo W. Leslie Good, per W. T. Stubbs

Left:
The 'Sandringhams' take over. 'B17' No 2806 *Audley End* waits with the up 'Continental' at Sheffield Victoria on 4 May 1929. The huge pile of coal on the tender will be noted. *Photo W. Leslie Good, per W. T. Stubbs*

Top:
'B17' No 2807 *Blickling* starts away from Sheffield with the up 'Continental' on 14 September 1929.
Photo W. Leslie Good, per W. T. Stubbs

Above:
No 2807 *Blickling* is seen again on the up 'Continental', this time at Worksop about 1930.
Photo T. G. Hepburn/Rail Archive Stephenson

Top:
'D10' 'Directors' were used on the up 'Continental' in the same way as the GNR Atlantics. Here is one of the engines involved, No 5437 *Prince George*, leaving Sheffield Victoria on 14 September 1929 with an up London train. At this period it was based at Neasden.
Photo W. Leslie Good, per W. T. Stubbs

Above:
LNER pageantry at Ipswich. 'B17' No 2845 *The Suffolk Regiment* is seen at the Showground station on 22 June 1935, decorated for the naming ceremony. The ceremony was performed by Major-General Sir John Ponsonby of the Suffolk Regiment, and on the footplate were Driver E. N. Brown and Fireman W. H. Mortimer, Suffolk Regiment veterans. *Photo E. A. Payne*

Top right:
Now in regular service, No 2845 *The Suffolk Regiment* traverses the Durham Ox level crossing on its way into Lincoln with the down 'Continental' in 1937.
Photomatic

Centre right:
'K3' engines were used by Gorton on the 'Continental' from 1936, and here is one of the engines involved, No 3816 on Gorton Loco.
Photo W. Leslie Good, per W. T. Stubbs

Right:
'D9' No 5113 of Lincoln passes the York Holgate excursion platforms in 1929 on the down York portion of the 'North Country Continental'. *K. Hoole collection*

Above:
'B4s' were used by Lincoln Loco on the York portion, later on. B4 No 6103 is seen passing the York Holgate excursion platforms with the up train on 26 July 1937. *Gresley Society collection*

Below:
'Footballers' were used on the 'Continental' from 1936. No 2860 *Hull City* **is at Gorton Loco on 25 July 1937. Gorton fireman Bert Turner is seen on the footplate at right.** *Photo W. Leslie Good, per W. T. Stubbs*

II

Slip Coach Finale

'Eleven people were injured . . . when a slip coach crashed into the rear of its parent train at Woodford Halse on Thursday night of last week.

'The accident occurred . . . almost under the Eydon Road bridge, about half a mile from Woodford & Hinton Station. The train concerned was the LNER 6.20pm restaurant car express from Marylebone to Bradford. It is the practice of this train to slip a coach at Finmere for Brackley, and another at Woodford Halse, the major portion of the train continuing its journey non-stop to Leicester.'

The *Rugby Advertiser*,
Friday 27 December 1935

The above extract is taken from a newspaper report of an accident which has since passed into Great Central folklore, and which in one important respect may be considered to mark the end of an era. Following official investigation of the accident the two slip portions referred to were withdrawn and replaced by stops, and so a long-established practice came to an end.

The history of slipping on the GCR goes back well into the 19th century, although it gradually declined after 1900. The peak year for slip operation was 1894, when the MSLR advertised no fewer than 11 separate slip portions. The total fell steadily after that, despite the fact that this was very much the heyday of slipping; companies such as the Great Western, for example, continued to offer a huge variety of slip services during these years, until eventually the practice was curtailed during World War 1. When peace returned most companies chose not to revive their slip services, and initially this was true of the GCR; then, somewhat tardily, they had second thoughts, and between 1920 and Grouping introduced two slip coaches, the latter actually coming into operation on the very day of Grouping, Monday 1 January 1923, and thus representing one of the last independent acts of the old company. Despite the lapse of time since similar services had operated, one at least was a recognisable descendant of prewar slip services.

The mainspring behind the introduction of these facilities, as in former times, was competition with that most powerful of rivals, the Great Western. By some quirk of railway geography it had come

about that the GCR was in possession of the shortest route between London and the important town of Stratford-on-Avon, and the only other company which could offer a competing service was the GWR. The old GCR service had therefore been trimmed down to offer smart and competitive times, and the Stratford services were made much of in the company's skilful advertising of pre-1914 days. During these enterprising years no fewer than four through Stratford coaches were provided, one of which was slipped at Woodford; it was this which, in little altered form, was to appear regularly in LNER timetables up to its withdrawal in 1936.

To reach Stratford the Great Central had of course to obtain running powers over 'foreign' metals, and the vital link was provided by a small company known as the Stratford-on-Avon & Midland Junction Railway (SMJR). The main line of this little-known system formed a lengthy cross-country connection between the LNWR main line at Blisworth and the Birmingham-Cheltenham line of the Midland Railway at Broom Junction; in between it served some of the quietest parts of Northamptonshire and Warwickshire, and Stratford-on-Avon was virtually the only town of any importance that it reached. Naturally, the SMJR advertised itself as 'The Shakespeare Route'. The small line would have had little or no importance for the GCR but for the fact that it happened to cross the Marylebone main line on an overbridge just south of Woodford; physical connection was easily provided by a northward-facing curve into Woodford, and the GCR had its much-desired access to Stratford. So attractive had the latter seemed as a source of revenue that in early days a south curve had also been built, enabling trains to run directly on and off the SMJR without calling at Woodford, but this was severed before the end of 1900 after falling into disuse and was afterwards utilised as a siding. Through coaches for Stratford reversed at Woodford after that date and ran via the north curve, which became known among local railwaymen as the 'Nibble'.

Links between the GCR and the small SMJR went considerably beyond those of physical proximity. Several prominent figures in SMJR affairs were connected in one way or another with the Great Central, such as Harry Willmott for example, sometime general manager of the LDECR which was absorbed into the GCR in 1907; he shared business interests with GCR

Chairman Sir Alexander Henderson and also with his son, Eric Butler-Henderson. Willmott eventually became Chairman of the SMJR. Other influential figures who no doubt encouraged the prospect of through working to and from London were Lord Willoughby de Broke, whose home was at Compton Verney a short distance from the SMJR line, and Ludford Docker, who resided in Stratford. Both were directors of the SMJR.

The postwar revival of slip working began in the spring of 1920, and there is reference in the *Railway Magazine* to the experimental slipping of a coach off the 3.15pm Marylebone-Manchester express during April[1]. In the following month the slip was transferred to the evening Bradford express, then departing from Marylebone at 6.10, and this vehicle, slipped at Brackley a few miles south of Woodford, was to remain in the timetables until September 1921.

Although slipped at a different station from prewar days, this coach provided the same through service to Stratford, being taken forward to Woodford on a local train and then going via the 'Nibble' to be attached to the rear of an SMJR train at neaby Byfield. The decision to slip at Brackley was probably governed by the expectation of more business as this town was considerably larger than Woodford, and of course the coach called at the latter anyway.

The fact that the Brackley slip survived for only a year and five months may be explained on the grounds that the anticipated custom failed to materialise, but there may have been a quite different reason; the Brackley slip was released on the 62ft-high viaduct a short distance south of the station, and in the event of malfunctioning of brakes on either the slip coach or its parent train there was a clear danger to passengers, especially in darkness or bad weather. Nothing has been traced to suggest that an accident involving the slip coach actually took place, but perhaps there was an occurrence which acted as a warning to the management. At all events, the Brackley slip was withdrawn from the timetable, as related, in September 1921.

It was immediately replaced by a still more familiar reminder of former practices, for the October timetable contained the announcement that the Bradford express would now slip at Woodford, as in the old days. The express was also retimed to leave Marylebone at 6.20pm, enabling the slip carriage to reach Woodford at 7.42pm and Stratford at 8.37pm. The overall journey time of 2 hours 17 minutes from Marylebone compared favourably with the best GWR trains from Paddington, although there was not more than a few minutes in it.

In order to attach the slip coach promptly to the Stratford train, an unusual manoeuvre took place

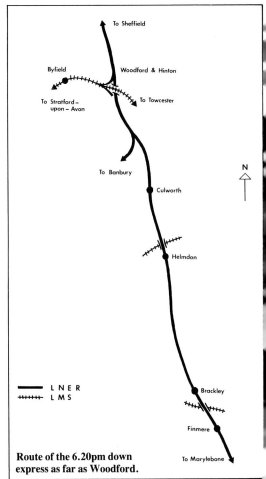

Route of the 6.20pm down express as far as Woodford.

whereby the SMJR train, reaching Byfield at 7.13pm after leaving Blisworth at 6.30pm backtracked along the 'Nibble' into Woodford and waited there fully 24 minutes before the slip coach eventually came to rest in the adjacent main platform. Passengers who happened to be travelling direct from Blisworth to Stratford were thus made well aware of the rather leisurely nature of 'Shakespeare Route' services, since the whole process of reversing into Woodford and attaching the slip coach consumed the better part of 50 minutes before the train arrived back again at Byfield to continue its way westward.

For travellers making the through journey from Marylebone to Stratford the contrast between the two systems must have been a striking one. The 6.20pm Bradford express was one of the fastest on the Great Central, beaten to Leicester only by the crack 'Sam Fay Down', and from 1929 by another flier, 'Promptitude'[2]; reaching Woodford non-stop in the very short space of 1 hour 22 minutes, the traveller now found himself grinding slowly round he curve of the 'Nibble' on a train that would call at all stations between Byfield and Stratford.

From a locomotive point of view the contrast was equally marked. The 6.20pm was among the cream of Leicester Loco workings, and it took care to turn out nothing less than its most powerful passenger engines, which by the post-World War 1 era were 'C4' Atlantics, formerly used by Gorton on crack workings of GCR days. With every nut and rivet gleaming from the attentions of the cleaners, these handsome machines proceeded to whirl the equally spotless train northward, but when the slip carriage eventually glided into Woodford it found itself attached to a very modest train of typical country branch appearance, headed in the post-Grouping era by an equally modest 0-6-0 engine. Once the contractor-built SMJR locomotives had been replaced, the Stratford service was operated by engines of Johnson origin, the line having of course been absorbed into the LMS, and thus did the intrepid Marylebone-Stratford traveller patronise two systems. The LMS flavour was increased, for a time, by the use of former LYR engines.

The SMJR owned quite a substantial installation at Stratford, including engine shed, goods yard and a number of sidings, but the passenger station was not large, consisting simply of two wayside platforms. Arriving at this somewhat quiet spot on the outskirts of the town, the empty slip carriage remained undisturbed in the down platform, still attached to its train, until the arrival of a train from Broom Junction at 9.15pm. The empty coaches of this were then shunted over onto the down train and the whole assembly complete with slip coach was deposited in the carriage sidings nearby. Here was a contrast with GCR practice, for it was an almost invariable rule that main-line stock not in use should be stored under cover; alas no such amenity as a carriage shed existed at Stratford, nor was there the usual army of cleaners waiting to warm over the vehicles, as was the custom on the GCR. The slip coach would not receive these ministrations until its return to Marylebone the next day.

Coming into operation on Monday 1 January 1923, the Finmere slip was obviously a last-minute innovation on the part of the Great Central. By comparison with the Woodford slip its daily diagram was a straightforward affair – taken forward to Brackley after release from the parent train, it was transferred smartly to an up stopping train and was back in London before the evening was out.

Unlike the Woodford coach, it could claim no parentage in pre-1914 days. No slip carriage had

ever been timetabled for Finmere before: archetype of the English wayside station and set in exquisitely rural surroundings, it was fated like most of its kind to see the passage of far more trains than ever called there. It was not even particularly convenient for the village it served, as Finmere itself lay a good mile away along the Oxford-Buckingham road, and the reader may well wonder why the GCR should choose such an unlikely venue for its slip operations. The answer, in the main, can be summed up in one familiar word – competition.

Only five miles or so down the road in the opposite direction to Finmere lay the small town of Bicester, positioned neatly astride the Paddington-Birmingham main line of the GWR. By 1922 Bicester was the fortunate recipient of two daily slips from London, and as the Great Central management was well aware, such luxury would never have been considered had this location not offered a market for such operations. In fact the whole area was liberally sprinkled with wealthy and influential commuters, residing in country houses or living the life of gentlemen farmers, and so towards the end of 1922 the GCR decided that it was high time to get into the act. Among its potential customers were such people as the Hon Louis Fleischmann, a banker who farmed at Chetwode Manor; Admiral Roger Keyes, hero of the 1918 Zeebrugge raid, who lived at Tingewick; Captain Ferrass Loftus of Tingewick Hall; Major Joliffe from The Grange, and a Captain Lindsay. Even more important than all these, probably, was the resident of Barton Hartshorn Manor, a mansion lying almost within sight of Finmere Station; he was none other than Colonel Charles William Trotter CB, formerly Chairman of the Hull & Barnsley Railway, latterly a director of the NER, and of the LNER following Grouping. No doubt Colonel Trotter was active in encouraging the introduction of the slip, and may have been the first to suggest the idea. Like the other gentlemen mentioned, he travelled daily to the city and was soon in the habit of returning home by the slip, which deposited him in record time at Finmere.

The daily appearance of these important gentlemen became part of the regular routine at Finmere, because after having been invited into the booking-office one cold morning to enjoy the comfort of the fire, they got into the habit of waiting there regularly. It appears that their presence was resented by the clerical staff, but one imagines that the porters and others on the platform were fairly quick to attend to the gentlemen in the hope of picking up a tip.

Other factors reinforced the decision to operate the Finmere slip. During 1923 an important educational establishment opened its doors at Stowe, just a few miles away across the fields from

Finmere; this was Stowe Public School, which welcomed its first pupils during that year. Over the years the scholars and staff of the school were to provide regular custom for Finmere station, and no doubt for its slip carriage. There was also the town of Buckingham, five miles away from Finmere; though it could claim a station of its own, this was on the unimportant Banbury branch off the LNWR Oxford-Cambridge line, and it could not rival the GCR line as a quick and direct means of access to London. At one period the GCR had advertised Finmere station as Finmere for Buckingham.

In retrospect it is clear that the decision to introduce the Finmere slip was a sound one, for after its commencement on that fateful first Monday of January 1923 the service was destined to remain in the timetable right through to withdrawal of the slips in 1936.

The slip carriages used were Nos 50177 and 50197 of 1911 vintage, built at Dukinfield. They had the characteristic rounded outline of GCR passenger vehicles of that period, and as this style was perpetuated on all passenger coaches subsequently built at Dukinfield, their appearance harmonised with the rest of the Bradford express on which they were marshalled each evening. After the introduction of Gresley-type stock in 1929 however, they stood out in stark contrast at the back of the train.

Such distinguished personages as Colonel Trotter and his companions invariably travelled first class, and so the slip carriages were necessarily composite vehicles, the two first-class compartments sandwiched together in the middle by the third-class accommodation on either side. This central position gave the smoothest ride because of its distance from the carrying bogies, and it was also the safest part of the vehicle in the event of a collision. The first-class accommodation was separated from the rest of the car by toilets on both sides, these thus forming a cordon sanitaire, if one may use that term, which reduced to a minimum any noise and disturbance from the less gentlemanly parts of the train. There were four toilet compartments altogether, including separate ones for each of the first class compartments.

At each end of the coach, embracing all, were small brake compartments housing the slipping-gear. By 1923 the mechanical arrangements were not quite as they had been originally, for vacuum reservoirs had been fitted which allowed the guard to halt the vehicle by using the normal brake instead of by the handbrake as at first. In other respects the coaches entered LNER service exactly as built.

When the stock for the 6.20pm Bradford express was brought into Marylebone's Platform 4 from the carriage sidings, the slip vehicles were of course at the rear, with the Finmere coach nearest the buffer stops. The main train guard, whose compartment was in the next vehicle but one, then took his place on the platform as it was his responsibility to ensure that all passengers were accommodated in the correct portions of the train – by no means an easy matter in the days before loudspeaker announcing had begun. Passengers were notified of the arrangements as they came through the barrier, but the guard remained on hand to give further assistance, and before departure made a last check by walking the full length of the train making enquiries.

Leicester-based guards were in charge of the main train, and the job was covered by a link of about 14 men, each working the turn in weekly rotation. Marylebone men were in charge of the slips, a link of five guards working the two jobs in conjunction with normal main-line duties. Compared with the latter the slip turns involved an added degree of responsibility, for satisfactory slipping ultimately depended on the guard's skill and experience.

The Finmere guard booked on duty earlier than his opposite number as he was responsible for testing the brakes and slipping-gear on both coaches before departure, a task which he carried out with the assistance of a shunter. To counterbalance their extra responsibilities, the slip guards had comparatively little to do in the way of dealing with luggage. London men known to have worked the slip turns between the wars included Frank Chorlton, Sam Dodds, Charles Robertson, Joe Hilton, Charles Murrell, Jack Swatton, Joe Donner and A. Robbins.

The Finmere slip was normally detached at the station distant signal, and its companion near the site of the Woodford & Hinton South Box, which had been demolished before Grouping. Before releasing the coach, the slip guard's first task was to part the vacuum brake pipe, which was done by pulling a cord; the pipes were fitted with special adaptors containing brass plug cocks which closed to seal the ends of the pipes when the cord was pulled. The guard then operated the release mechanism, which consisted of a second cord attached to a spring lock; a tug on the cord opened the lock and allowed a hinged shackle to separate and release the drawhook. The train heating pipes were self-sealing and were designed to part under tension as the slip coach dropped away. The slip guard was now in full control of his vehicle and responsible for bringing it safely to rest in the station. Appropriate signals were conveyed to the enginemen – a green flag or lamp was shown by the train guard when slipping was completed, a red

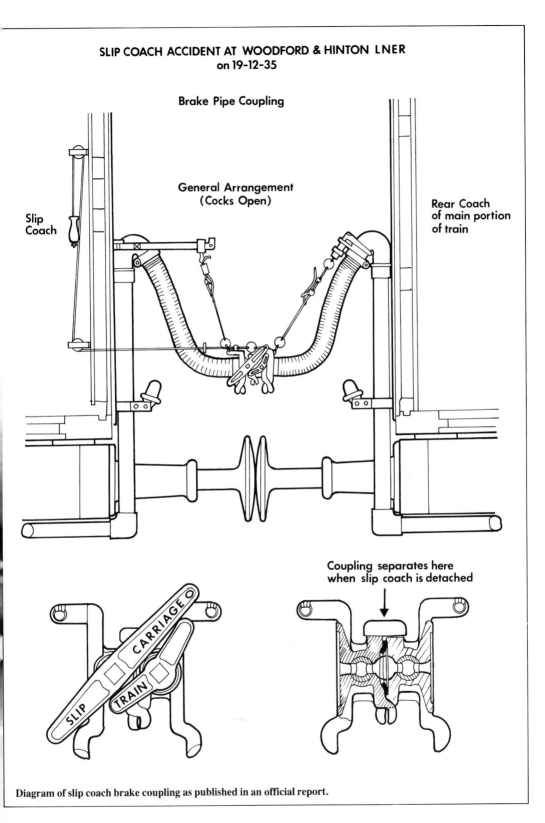

SLIP COACH ACCIDENT AT WOODFORD & HINTON LNER
on 19-12-35

Brake Pipe Coupling

General Arrangement
(Cocks Open)

Slip
Coach

Rear Coach
of main portion
of train

Coupling separates here
when slip coach is detached

CARRIAGE

SLIP TRAIN

Diagram of slip coach brake coupling as published in an official report.

one by the slip guard if for any reason slipping could not be carried out; both were acknowledged by the engine whistle. In the latter event the driver halted his train at the station so that the slip coach could be detached. Upon arrival it was the slip guard's responsibility to remove the special adaptor from the end of the brake pipe and place it in a box provided in his compartment; after arrival back at Marylebone this was checked for defects by a carriage and wagon examiner and then placed in the stationmaster's office until required for the next journey. The guard's final task was to lock the slip compartment so as to safeguard the mechanism from any possibility of tampering.

Reasonable visibility was essential for slipping, and if bad weather prevailed in the vicinity of the slip destinations it was up to the respective stationmasters to use their discretion as to whether or not slipping could be safely carried out. If they decided against it a wire had to be sent to Marylebone not later than 6pm, and written instructions were then handed to the enginemen and guards. Should bad weather set in after an 'all right' start, a message was sent to the signalbox in advance of the point of slipping and the train was halted for verbal instructions. Cancellation of the slips was unpopular with the enginemen as the stops which replaced them added considerably to the difficulties of what was already one of the hardest locomotive assignments on the GCR main line. In actual fact cancellation seems to have been very rare; Stationmaster H. Gardner of Woodford & Hinton claimed that in the years 1931-36 he had occasion to cancel the Woodford slip only twice, and no doubt much the same could be said of Finmere.[3] The Great Central was proud of its reputation for punctuality, and it is clear that such decisions were taken only with great reluctance. On the very few occasions that cancellation took place the slip guards still travelled in the usual way in order to be on hand for their return workings.

The Finmere slip was booked to arrive at 7.28pm, and waiting for it at the station was the engine and single coach which had arrived as the 6.30pm slow train from Woodford. This quaint assembly attracted attention in the railway press at one period because of the curious contrast between the solitary coach and the large and powerful engine in charge, one of Woodford's 'B7' 4-6-0s doing a fill-in turn before a goods working. The slip was quickly attached at the rear and the 'B7' returned at 7.32pm, complete with its two coaches and now running tender-first as there were of course no turning facilities at a small station such as Finmere. Reaching Brackley, the slip was swiftly transferred to the 7.59pm Brackley-High Wycombe stopping train, on which it ran as an ordinary coach with the slip compartments locked. From High Wycombe it was worked forward with the rest of the train as empty stock. The 7.59pm from Brackley was of some interest in that it was hauled by a Class A5 tank working one of Neasden Loco's longest suburban diagrams. Over the year the time varied slightly, and during the 1930s the empty stock turn from High Wycombe became an advertised train reaching Marylebone at 10.38pm.

After its overnight stay at Stratford, the Woodford slip carriage set off back to London in somewhat grander style. Marshalled as part of the 7.45am Stratford-Blisworth train, it stood adjacent to a platform indicator board that proudly proclaimed 'Through Train to London', staff being on hand to ensure that all London-bound passengers duly boarded it. The pretentious 'Through Train' label was however somewhat belied by its subsequent progress, as in typical SMJR style it duly called at all stations; milk was picked up at Ettington, Kineton and Fenny Compton and it eventually reached Byfield exactly an hour later. Here it was met by the engine and coach of the 8.37am passenger from Woodford, to which the through coach was quickly attached for an arrival in Woodford at 8.57am. Typical GCR smartness characterised the next manoeuvre; the up Mansfield express was already slowing for the Woodford stop as the through coach drew to rest and by 9.08 was on its way to Marylebone with the latter attached. Arrival at Marylebone was at 10.48am, the overall time of over three hours being considerably longer than in the down direction. After being released, the slip carriage was taken to the adjacent sheds for cleaning and remarshalling with the parent train in readiness for the next evening's departure.

Comparing up and down journeys, the reader will have noticed a difference in the way that the slip was transferred between Woodford and Byfield. In the down direction, as described earlier, it was attached directly to the LMS train and taken to Byfield by the same engine which continued through to Stratford. On the return journey however it was worked by the LNER engine which had come to Byfield on the 8.42am arrival. This particular turn was diagrammed for one of the Woodford pilots – the up side goods pilot at one period in the 1920s, and latterly the passenger pilot. No definite information has been traced as to what type of engine worked these duties at particular periods, but the most likely choice would be Class N5; an observer visiting the district at some unspecified date in the mid-1930s saw two of the class, Nos 5767 and 5900, at Byfield. There were no turning facilities at the latter, and clearly tank engines would be preferred on the various trips made over the 'Nibble'.

During the early years of the LNER a slip carriage was based permanently at Woodford and worked a short daily diagram to Banbury and back. In all probability this vehicle would have been one of the six slip coaches built at Gorton in 1903, and was presumably retained as a spare in the event of either of the regular coaches being out of use. In later years this coach, or a similar one, was working on Marylebone-Sudbury Hill locals.

Despite the existence of a spare vehicle great efforts were made to keep the regular coaches in tip-top condition. Like all main-line passenger carriages they receive meticulous attention when in the sheds – couplings and springs were thoroughly checked, axleboxes were topped up, accumulators, dynamos and other electrical equipment were examined, and the coach itself thoroughly cleaned and polished inside and out. The carriage sheds were equipped to deal with all but the most serious defects, and night shifts were worked so that stock could be got ready for morning expresses. All this endeavour was considered more than worthwhile for its advertisement value alone – the cleaner the coaches, the better the impression on the public; its main purpose of course was to ensure, as far as possible, freedom from failure on the road. The only real lapse in this regular routine affected the Woodford coach during its weekend stay at Stratford; as there were no Sunday return workings to Marylebone, it had perforce to remain at Stratford for over 36 hours.

Mileage of all coaches was always carefully checked, and main-line workings rotated so that as far as possible all sets of stock worked the same distance. In the case of the slip carriages this meant that the two workings would be changed over from time to time, probably on a weekly basis.

After more than 13 years of regular running under LNER auspices, the Great Central slip services were withdrawn early in 1936. This development was clearly the result of the accident at Woodford referred to at the beginning of this chapter, and in view of their importance in GC section history these events are worth looking at in some detail.

The accident took place on Thursday 19 December 1935 in the darkness of a winter's evening, and it was fortunate that the collision involving the slip coach was not an exceptionally violent one as the vehicle was rather more crowded than usual, the additional passengers being Christmas shoppers who had spent the day in London. Their injuries were fairly slight, and the only serious casualties were the two guards.

On the evening in question the train consisted of eight vehicles, weighing about 290 tons all told – a somewhat above average load for the period, and considerably so by the standards of early LNER days, when GCR expresses had often comprised only five coaches or less. The engine was one of the usual 'C4' Atlantics from Leicester Loco, No 6086, and the crew was Driver Ernie Cawkwell and Fireman R. W. Elliott, both of the Leicester Top Link. The engine and men had worked into London in the usual way on the 3pm arrival from Bradford, which they had taken over at Leicester. A generous turn-round time was allowed on this diagram so that the engine could be thoroughly prepared for the very testing return trip. The main train guard was Dick Bonnett of Leicester, with Charles Robertson in the Woodford slip; the identity of the Finmere guard has not been accurately recorded, although Guard A. Robbins is mentioned in the *Rugby Advertiser* account of the accident.

At Culworth Junction, three miles south of Woodford, the train was running several minutes behind time, and although there were fog patches about the train does not appear to have suffered delay from this cause. Perhaps the task of keeping time on this difficult working was proving just a little too much for the Atlantic; by the end of 1935 these engines were on average 30 years old – No 6086 was almost exactly that age – and the kind of work required on the evening Bradford turn was considerably more arduous than what they had been used to. By Culworth Junction the Finmere carriage had already been slipped in the normal way, and we may picture No 6068 speeding through the night at anything up to 70mph, or perhaps more if Driver Cawkwell was making any attempt to pull back time.

At this point Guard Robertson would have been getting ready to make the slip, and it was as he began to do this that the vital malfunction occurred. When he pulled the cord to seal the ends of the brake pipe the cock on the train portion failed to close properly, and directly the two pipes separated the brakes on the main train began to leak on. Quite unaware of this, he released the slip mechanism in the normal way. In the main train, Guard Bonnett was also unaware of what was happening, depite the vacuum gauge in his compartment, and gave the appropriate green signal to the enginemen as the slip coach dropped away. Unfortunately, exhaust steam from the hardworking engine prevented the crew from seeing this signal, and they assumed that for some reason the slip had not been made, and that the guard had simply applied the brake in order to carry out the alternative procedure by stopping the train at Woodford. When it became apparent that the train was stopping in advance of the station, Driver Cawkwell must have begun to realise that something was amiss, but with the brake fully on he was powerless to prevent his train from coming to a stand. Approaching the now stationary train from the rear, Guard Robertson was unable to see the red tail-light because of steam drifting back, and so could do nothing to avert the resulting collision, which occurred at an estimated speed of 20mph.

Passengers were thrown against the bulkheads and were lucky to escape with minor injuries and bruises, but Guards Robertson and Bonnett were both badly hurt as the two brake compartments came into direct contact, taking the full force of the impact. The underframe of the slip carriage overrode that of the train vehicle by several feet, and both coaches suffered extensive damage.

To establish the cause of the accident, tests with a special train were required, and these took place on Thursday 2 January 1936 as part of the Ministry of Transport enquiry, with the same crew in charge of the engine. It was established that the accident had been caused by the brake pipe cock failing to close, but despite close study of the slipping procedure during the tests the inspecting officer was unable to say exactly why this had happened. In the subsequently published report he offered two possible reasons – first, that as the two sets of cocks parted company, the main train cock had not been fully closed and a small external lever attached to it had struck a projection on the coach body as it fell, knocking the cock wide open; secondly, that because of tension on the brake-pipe hoses the sets of cocks had sprung apart too quickly for the cocks to close, and that the resulting jerk had closed the cock on the slip coach, but not the one on the train.

In either event the inspecting officer was bound to be critical of the brake-pipe equipment, especially as similar though less serious failures were found to have happened previously, and he had no option but to make unfavourable comparisons between the GCR pattern of brake cock and the improved type currently in use on the Great Western. He suggested that in view of the excellent GWR safety record, the LNER authorities should make use of apparatus similar to that employed by the former.

Publication of the MoT report was delayed until March because the two guards were not sufficiently recovered to give evidence, and long before then the LNER had carried out its own investigation and, no doubt, come to its own definite conclusions as to the cause of the accident. This inquiry was held on the day after the accident and, in all probability, the decision to suspend slipping was taken as a result of the findings. According to official sources, slipping ceased with effect from Saturday 1 February 1936, but the service may well have been suspended before this date.

The termination of slipping meant that stops had to be introduced into the schedule of the 6.20pm express, with the result that it was considerably slowed down; this change came at a time when many services elsewhere were being accelerated and so it hardly constituted good publicity for the GCR section. The slower schedule was not apparent at Finmere, where the express was now booked to stop just slightly in front of the former slip-coach time, but at Woodford there was a difference of two minutes, and this had widened to five minutes at Leicester, with the train now arriving at 8.19pm instead of 8.14pm. Nevertheless, the extremely smart station work on the GCR was still very much in evidence, for at Woodford the through coach to Stratford was detached in the space of one minute. At Finmere passengers could still continue to Brackley as before, but now had to change into another coach.

Despite the easier schedule, the working of the 6.20 was still a stiff proposition from a locomotive point of view, and within a short time of the slip coaches being withdrawn the elderly 'C4' Atlantics were replaced by 'B17' 'Footballers'[4]. The last recorded working of an Atlantic was on Friday 21 February 1936, when No 5363 was in charge, driven by Leicester's Tom Newall.

Thus ended slipping on the GC section. Limited to two portions operated with unmodernised vehicles, the practice during LNER days could hardly be described as much more than a modest remnant of former times, and in some respects it is surprising that it lasted as long as it did. It could well have disappeared as early as 1926, for during April of that year there was an occurrence at Finmere which bears a distinct resemblance to the accident of 1935. Immediately after the slip coach had been released, the engine crank-axle fractured and the train was brought to a halt, but luckily it finished up far enough away for the slip portion to reach the station in safety. Little is known of this incident, but the engine is believed to have been Class C5 Atlantic No 5259 *King Edward VII*, which was in Gorton Works for a repair during May 1926 after having received a general overhaul only a very short time before.

The GC section slip workings illustrate a tendency on the part of the LNER to leave Great Central passenger services very much as they found them in 1923, with comparatively few changes being made either in timetable or equipment. The introduction of Gresley-type coaches on to the GCR line in the spring of 1929 might be thought to have offered an opportunity for reviewing the future of the slip service, but no consideration appears to have been given to this. In common with all Gresley vehicles, the new coaches had a central vestibule, and in order to make a brake connection with the following slip ortion it was necessary to provide an extra length of brake hose positioned to one side of the vestibule; hence the brake connection ahead of the Woodford coach was somewhat differently arranged than that between the two slips, and it was the opinion of the inspecting officer that this probably contributed to the accident of 1935.

Notes

1 C. J. Allen, 'British Locomotive Practice & Performance', *Railway Magazine*.
2 Jackson & Russell, *The Great Central in LNER Days*, Chapter 7.
3 1936 Ministry of Transport Report, Woodford & Hinton Accident.
4 Jackson & Russell, *The Great Central in LNER Days*, Chapter 5.

Above:
Woodford station in BR days, looking north. Originally Woodford & Hinton, it had been renamed Woodford Halse by the time this picture was taken. *Photo BR*

Below:
'C4' No 6086 was the engine involved in the Woodford accident of 1935. Here it is seen in its prime as GCR No 1086, passing Whetstone on an up express. *Authors' collection*

Above:
The Stratford slip coach was conveyed back to London on the morning Mansfield-Marylebone express, which is seen here approaching South Ruislip with an unidentified 'C4' Atlantic at the head.
Photomatic

Below:
Driver Ted Simpson of Neasden, nearest the camera, in the cab of 'B3' No 6167 in August 1940. He drove the train which conveyed the MoT inspecting officer and railway officials to Woodford to investigate the accident there, the engine on that occasion being a 'Director'.
Photo R. H. N. Hardy

III

'Passengers for Glossop and Hadfield!'

'The later Great Central suburban stock, high, wide and handsome . . . was easily the best in Great Britain. . . A suburban train servicing all stations from Manchester London Road to Glossop was a very different thing from that between Marylebone and Aylesbury.'

C. Hamilton Ellis, *The Trains We Loved*, Allen & Unwin, 1947.

Any comparison between the Marylebone suburban trains and those serving Glossop and Hadfield, such as that quoted above, is likely to err on the side of understatement, and this one is no exception. The Glossop and Hadfield trains were indeed a very different thing from almost every possible point of view, so much so that it is difficult to find similarities beyond the fact that both services performed the same basic function of taking city workers to and from their offices. Some of the most obvious differences arose out of historical factors; because the Glossop service had been established over long years, as opposed to its southern counterpart where the GCR had done everything it could to capture new business, the locomotives and coaches used on the former were significantly smaller and older, the coaches particularly so. There was certainly nothing high, wide or handsome, to quote C. Hamilton Ellis again, about the gaslit six-wheelers which made up

most of the Glossop trains, and they offered a standard of comfort which was a very far cry from that enjoyed by the commuters of Aylesbury or High Wycombe. Nor did the limited comfort derive purely from the design of the coaches: the less congenial northern climate also had its effect during the winter, when it was common for passengers to be left shivering in poorly heated compartments while the trains were delayed because of snow or fog, or because the heavy main-line service had been disrupted. A further contrast could also be descried in the locomotive types used: at Marylebone the suburban trains were handled exclusively by the large and modern Class A5 engines, of which the most recent examples had been built during the 1920s, whereas the Glossop trains were usually worked by the 'F1' 2-4-2 tanks, very much smaller than their London counterparts and originally designed in the late 19th century. On these grounds alone it can safely be said that no other railway company in Britain operated two such vastly dissimilar steam-worked suburban services as did the Great Central at the northern and southern ends of its system.

A further marked contrast is to be seen in the social background to the two traffics. Glossop and Hadfield, together forming the municipal borough of Glossop, were totally different in character from the towns on the Marylebone suburban lines. In the main, the latter were fairly typical commuter settlements, having grown up round what had formerly been villages and small country towns as former city dwellers moved further and further out

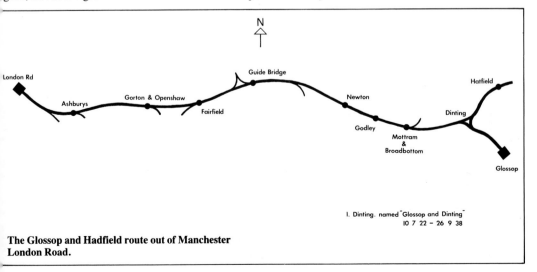

The Glossop and Hadfield route out of Manchester London Road.

into the open spaces. This trend was of course much influenced by the existence of good rail facilities, and the populations of these places were in most cases rising steadily during the years which this book covers. By contrast, Glossop at about 1930 could not by any stretch of the imagination have been described as town people by emigrants from Manchester. It was at that time a totally self-contained settlement, owing almost its entire existence to the rise of the cotton trade during the 19th century, and from the Great War onwards showed a population trend exactly the opposite to that of Aylesbury or High Wycombe, the result of the postwar slump and general decline in the textile industries. Because of this, a small number of residents were beginning to find work either in Manchester or one of the neighbouring towns served by the railway line (although from the beginning of 1928 Stalybridge and Ashton-under-Lyne were more easily reached by bus), but by far the majority of those travelling daily to Manchester and its vicinity in the 1930s were people from a slightly more advantaged background who had been able to obtain employment of a clerical or semi-clerical nature in the city, in preference to working in the traditional weaving and textile printing industries; this group found a wide range of opportunities in Manchester, working in the wholesale and cotton warehouses of the city centre, in the Town Hall or offices of the Civil Service. Others were employed by such large concerns as the Co-operative Wholesale Society, principally at its head office in Balloon Street, the Co-operative Insurance Society and the Refuge Assurance Company, and there were also many shop workers employed at large stores such as Lewis's, Marks & Spencer's, Affleck & Brown's, Henry's, and a wide variety of other shops large and small.

Because of the relatively small number of true commuters, the Glossop and Hadfield service did not have the obvious peaks that were to be found in the more typical of such local services; several trains left Hadfield in the morning within a fairly short time of each other, balancing a similar exodus from London Road every evening, but on the whole the service was evenly spread throughout the day. Nor was there much in the way of change over the years, in contrast to what happened on the southern services.

An unusual feature of the service was that the trains themselves varied considerably in character. Most of the true locals, for want of a better term, were made up of sets of stock plying between Glossop, Hadfield and London Road on a variety of working diagrams. Mixed in with these were trains working between Manchester and Sheffield or sometimes even further afield which called at Glossop en route, or if they did not actually work

along the branch were booked to stop at eithe Dinting or Hadfield, or both. Thirdly there was th Glossop branch train, making connection a Dinting either with the main-line trains ju described, or with locals which did not work alon the branch into Glossop. Readers not familiar wit the district may find this description easier t follow by consulting the plan of the branch.

Taking these various elements into account, th service was quite lavish, and considerably superio to its postwar counterpart of pre-electrificatio days, which never recovered from the wartim cuts. This is surprising when one considers that i the 1930s the number of people using the train was probably smaller. Furthermore, because of th inclusion of the fast train connections at Dinting the average journey time was higher than in late years, though it is only fair to add that most of th ordinary locals were very slow by the standards o the 1954 electrification, taking 50 minutes or mor if calling at all stations.

The many peculiarities of the Glossop servic were to a large extent the product of the triangula junction at Dinting which had been put in durin the 1880s. In the days when the junction had consisted simply of an east-facing curve on to th main line, passengers had invariably travelled t and from Glossop on the branch train, changing a Dinting in both directions, but once the new junction had been put in, this simple system gave way to a remarkable complexity of workings Trains arriving at Glossop (or Glossop Central t use its correct 1930s title) could be locals working directly in via Dinting, or they could have gone t Hadfield first and worked in from that direction Manchester-Sheffield main-line trains working into Glossop did so with the engine tender-first continuing chimney-first for the rest of the journey, while trains from Sheffield to Mancheste worked in chimney-first and out tender-first. Lastly there were the arrivals of the branch train not so frequent as in the early days, but still shuttling backwards and forwards to make its various connections at Dinting. Thus a passenger travelling from Manchester to Glossop might catch a local going directly along the branch, or change at Dinting if he caught a train going direct to Hadfield, while in the reverse direction it was necessary to change at Dinting on certain trains very few passengers travelled regularly in the Sheffield direction from Glossop. On a very small number of trains passengers for Glossop were set down at Dinting without any connection to Glossop being provided, which meant that they had to resort to the bus service; the nearest stop was some distance away however, and for many it was probably quicker to walk, certainly those heading for the western parts of the town. It may be mentioned that during these years Dinting was actually known as Glossop & Dinting, strictly speaking a more accurate name since the station lay within the borough boundaries; it was changed to Dinting shortly before the start of World War 2.

From a locomotive point of view the branch line could be used to advantage, for if an engine made only one trip to Glossop Central in the course of an out-and-home working from Manchester London Road, it could perform the whole turn chimney-first except for the short stretch between Glossop and Hadfield. Thus a diagram which included an outward working to Hadfield via the branch often provided for a direct return, avoiding a second trip into Glossop; as there were no turning facilities at either Glossop or Hadfield, and insufficient time to make use of them even if there had been, this meant that tender engines could still be used on the turns, even though in practice the trains were normally the preserve of 'F1', 'F2' and 'C13' tanks. Taking an example at random, the 8.40am local from London Road worked direct to Hadfield (no advertised connection for Glossop passengers at Dinting), reversed there in the somewhat generous time of 45 minutes to form the 8.05am to Manchester, which then travelled via Glossop, the engine returning to the chimney-first position when it ran round the train in Glossop Central.

The branch acted to the disadvantage of tender engines working beyond Hadfield, as there was no option but to run tender-first as far as Glossop; this applied for instance to the 4.19 arrival on Sunday afternoon, which at the beginning of the decade was an outward working for a Gorton engine, usually a 'B7', going to Grimsby in order to work back next day with a down fish train; later it became an Immingham turn[1]. During the 1920s there had been a similar working leaving London Road at 6.30pm, but by 1930 this had been re-routed to run direct via Dinting, passengers for Glossop changing into the branch train. Workings such as these always stood out at the Glossop end of the line because of the marked contrast between large tender types such as Class B7 and the usual 'tankies', to use the railwaymen's term for them.

In 1930 the local service proper was dominated by the Class F1 engines. This 2-4-2 design dated from Thomas Parker's time at Gorton, and the engines had now put in something approaching 40 years of service; they were nonetheless regarded as being still well capable of tackling the locals and were in many ways ideal machines for the job, since besides having a surprising turn of speed their short overall length made them easy to handle in the restricted confines of stations such as Glossop Central, and as with all GCR tank types the comfortable and roomy cab was much appreciated by footplate crews. Most of the 'F1s' had gone into service on the Manchester suburban

trains from new, and had never done anything else since, so that they became extremely familiar to residents of the Glossop district, whether regular rail travellers or not. Like all GCR engines they underwent a rather drastic change of chimney style after 1923, all of the class gradually losing their tapered Robinson chimneys in favour of a much more severe-looking style usually described as a 'flowerpot'. This change was already well under way by 1930 and is thought to have been completed about three years later. The replacement chimneys have come in for criticism in various writings, and it has been said that their ugliness ruined the formerly handsome appearance of these neat little tank engines; however, the shock effect of these chimneys gradually faded as more and more of the various tank engine classes acquired a type that was either identical or very similar, and in the end people seemed to get used to them, while some actually grew to like them.

Coaching stock of 1930 was mostly of the old-fashioned six-wheel types, marshalled in trains of about seven or eight vehicles, the sets being strengthened at busy times. The coaches were cramped and uncomfortable, and the gas lighting helped to create an atmosphere of unrelieved dinginess. The Glossop branch train of this period consisted of a split section of one of the normal sets, usually three vehicles. All stock was mainly based at Ardwick Carriage Sidings, situated just east of Ardwick station on the up side of the main line, but the carriage diagrams were arranged to allow sets of stock to finish their workings at Glossop and Hadfield in the evenings so that they could be used for the first trains out the next morning. Two sets of stock were deposited at Glossop Central every night, one stored in the Howard Street siding against the reverse face of the platform, the other on a road adjacent to the goods warehouse. A third set was left at Hadfield, parked in a siding east of the station on the up side of the line. Coaches remaining at Glossop over the weekend were normally left in the Howard Street siding throughout Sunday, so that the string of passenger vehicles at the side of the road became part of the local scenery.

With a very few exceptions the working of the local service was shared between Gorton and the small sub-shed at Dinting. The latter had no official engine allocation of its own, receiving its supply of motive power on a rotating basis from the parent shed. Engines normally remained at Dinting for about three weeks before returning to Gorton for washing-out, there being no facilities for this at the former. They were taken to Gorton at night, volunteer crews working them down light engine, and a replacement engine was brought back. Three

'F1s' took care of Dinting's passenger turns, assisted by a goods tender engine, usually a 'J11' 'Pom-Pom'. Together these were responsible for the early-morning departures for Manchester, while their counterparts at Gorton began the service from that end of the line. Most of the 'F1' engines were based at Gorton during LNER days, but unfortunately no records were ever kept of the sequence in which they were sent out to the various sub-sheds, and this was evidently done more or less on a random basis; it is therefore impossible to say which engines were employed on the Glossop services at any specific date.

Passenger activity at Glossop began on weekdays at 5.35am when Dinting's 'J11' arrived, fresh off the shed; this was the Glossop goods pilot, but in addition to its goods work it took charge of three passenger trips to Dinting and back during the course of the morning. During the winter months its arrival time was a little earlier in order to allow time for steam-heating the coaches. It attached itself to the rake of stock in the Howard Street road and set off for Dinting with the first three coaches, the set having been split in readiness for the working. This was an advertised connection for the 5.25am London Road-Sheffield train, but not surprisingly very few Glossop passengers have been recalled as having availed themselves of it, and the main purpose of the trip was to collect the newspapers and mail for Glossop which were unloaded in considerable quantities off the 5.25 train at Dinting. The work of transferring it all on barrows from the up main platform to the branch train waiting in No 3 has been described as very heavy, so much so that despite the allowance of 17 minutes at Dinting the return trip was frequently late. At about this time also, economies had been made in the Dinting platform staffing by which the man on early shift no longer had the assistance of a junior porter, as previously, and the early-turn platform man at Glossop was now booked to travel to Dinting on the 5.53am and assist with the transfer from the main line; this appears to have made little or no improvement to the timekeeping however, and it seems that it was not unknown for passengers to assist! These mainly consisted of several bus crews on their way to begin work at the Glossop depot of the North Western Road Car Co, anxious not to be late and for that reason more than willing to help the platform man shove the heavy barrow across the main line and up the ramp on to the branch platform, regardless of LNER rules about passengers using the bridge.

At Glossop the return arrival was awaited by a member of the local Post Office staff, complete with the regulation red-painted barrow for transporting the sacks of mail; with him was the town's newspaper wholesaler, a Mr Dale. At this period also there was a small dairy operating in Glossop, and the train's load included several churns of milk which had to be manhandled on to barrows to be taken to a waiting cart. While unloading was being done the goods pilot ran round its train, replacing the coaches on the Howard Street road in due course and then moving off to take up its duties in the adjacent goods yard.

The next activity was the arrival at 6.55am of the 6.50am from Hadfield. The Dinting men on the 'early turn passenger' had run light engine to Hadfield with an 'F1', leaving the shed at 6.15 in the warmer months and at about 5.45 in the winter in order to heat the coaches. Having coupled up the 'F1' stood for a considerable time in the siding as it was not allowed into the station until shortly before departure time because of the need to keep the main line clear. During the winter months a member of the platform staff was charged with the task of lighting up the stock, a time-consuming business if carried out in the regulation manner by going from compartment to compartment, and therefore usually done by walking along the carriage roofs and igniting the gas from above. On arrival at Glossop the train was allowed the usual five minutes for the engine to run round, and departed at 7am with the coaches well filled; its arrival in Manchester at 7.44 after calling at all stations allowed most passengers to reach their work by 8am, which in those days was a popular starting-time for office and warehouse staff.

As the train left Glossop, another 'F1' arrived from Dinting and backed on to the set of stock which had been parked adjacent to the goods warehouse; the stock was drawn out and propelled into the platform, and the assembly then made a trip to Dinting at 7.10am to connect with the 6.40am London Road-Hadfield train. Arriving back in Glossop at 7.28 it then formed the next Manchester departure, which left at 7.37 with the second batch of commuters. From the end of July 1932 the trip to Dinting was switched to Hadfield and the former 7.37am departure from Glossop now became the 7.25 ex-Hadfield, the Hadfield-Glossop leg of this forming the return working of the 7.10 trip. Both before and after these adjustments this train claimed the distinction of being the smartest of the morning trains from Glossop into the city, running non-stop beyond Guide Bridge and reaching London Road at 8.09am.

The 6.40am London Road-Hadfield train just mentioned worked to Glossop at 8.05 after a spell in the sidings at Hadfield and became the 8.14 to Manchester, taking out yet another trainload of city workers. The engine and coaches of this train were the first 'foreigners' of the day into Glossop as this was a Gorton turn with coaches from Ardwick. The return arrival of 8.46 in Manchester neant that this train could only be used by the more privileged group of workpeople whose starting-time was nine o'clock.

Finally there was the 8.33am arrival in Glossop, which was in many ways the most interesting of all. This train stood out in sharp contrast to earlier ones because of two very noticeable features – a different class of engine, and much better quality stock. It had also travelled much further; leaving Sheffield Victoria at 7.10am, it had worked over Woodhead, calling at all stations – the only train of the day that did so in the down direction. In charge were Sheffield men from Neepsend's so-called 'Tanky Link', aboard an engine that represented a definite advance in size and power over the 'F1s' which usually appeared on earlier trains, namely a 'C13'. As for the train, the substantial bogie stock was a marked contrast to the dingy six-wheelers which comprised the other trains, and the extra comfort was closely connected with the train's departure time, for only the most privileged and important of commuters could make regular use of a train that did not reach the city until 9.17am. Not surprisingly, the number of passengers using the 'eight thirty-eight', as it was known to Glossopians, was a good deal less than could be seen on earlier trains. A point of interest about the 8.38 is that at that time it was the only regular working into Glossop on which one could see a 'C13' tank, a class which became much more closely associated with the district in later years.

With this departure an extremely strenuous start to the day was brought to an end as far as the Glossop platform staff were concerned. Having come on duty at 5.30am, the first man on the shift had a whole variety of jobs to do in addition to his normal platform duties; these included lighting the fires in the booking office, waiting rooms and adjacent goods office, sweeping out the waiting rooms and mopping out the lavatories, as well as issuing tickets to passengers until the arrival of the booking-clerk towards 7am, and making the trip to Dinting and back for the papers and mails, as

described. As each train arrived he was responsible for uncoupling the engine, and then having scrambled back on to the platform had to operate the points to allow the engine to run round; he next had to transfer the tail-lamp to the appropriate end of the train as the engine backed up, and in addition carry out the porter's normal duties of assisting passengers and seeing that all doors were properly closed on departure. The last job was a particularly awkward one at Glossop as the doors closed in the direction that the train was travelling, instead of against it as was normally the case – with many passengers boarding at the last minute there was usually a need to close doors as the train was actually moving off. Furthermore it was doubly important that all doors should be closed properly as that side of the train was not used again during the journey to Manchester. The arrival of each train at Glossop therefore signified the start of a frantic race against time, and one which was not always won, as forms demanding explanations for platform delays were frequently circulated. With the tail of the 8.38 finally disappearing in the direction of Dinting, the hard-pressed platform hand could at last breathe a sigh of relief and retire to the porters' room for a well-earned breakfast, knowing that there would be no more heavy train work for the rest of the shift.

Platform work at the stations en route hardly compared in difficulty with the situation at Glossop, being mainly confined to the routine tasks of assisting passengers, closing doors, loading parcels and so on. However, at some places these jobs were not quite as easy as they became in later

Below:
Passenger arrangements at Glossop Central. Empty coaches were stored in what are described here as the 'Cattle Dock Siding' and 'Back Road Siding'. The station canopy is shown by the shaded area, and all incoming trains drew to a halt just clear of this, except for the push-and-pull, which went right up to the buffer-stops.

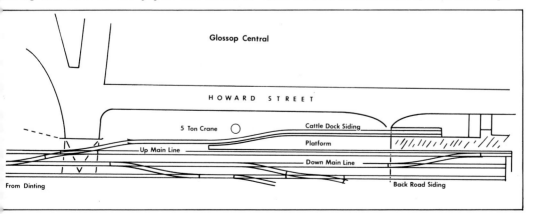

Glossop Central

HOWARD STREET

5 Ton Crane

Cattle Dock Siding

Platform

Up Main Line

Down Main Line

From Dinting

Back Road Siding

years because many station platforms were still in original condition, and therefore much lower than has become the norm in more recent times. With the compartment door open at such places, a porter of average height found that his head was about on a level with the knees of those seated inside, and this made platform work more difficult in certain respects. Stations which had the original low platforms were Hadfield, Mottram & Broadbottom, Godley and Newton. Ashburys and Ardwick had a mixture, the up platform in both cases being of the original type, while the single platform at Glossop was a curious concoction, most of it still in original condition but with a raised section towards the further end, evidently added on at a later date. Stations which had at some time been rebuilt, namely Glossop & Dinting, Guide Bridge, Fairfield, and Gorton & Openshaw, had the later type of platform.

The Dinting engines made further Manchester trips during the quieter part of the day and were remanned by the second shift men in the early afternoon, change-over of crews taking place at Dinting station. In 1930 the only Gorton working into the district during this period of the day was on the 10.05am departure from London Road, which ran direct to Hadfield and then returned via the branch, arriving in Glossop at 11 o'clock. At 11.20 a third Dinting engine came off the shed and worked trips on the branch until departing for Manchester at 4.42pm from Glossop Central. By this time the evening rush was about to get under way at the other end, and so it is convenient here to review the situation which existed in those days at Manchester London Road, especially as it displayed several unusual features.

Despite the considerable size of the establishment, the GCR share of London Road was a small one, comprising only three platforms located at the far left of the station as one faced Glossop. To avoid confusion with the adjacent LNWR platforms they were known by letters instead of the more usual numbers, with Platform A being at the extreme left; so far as is known this use of letters was unique to the Great Central. For train departures it was the practice to retain Platform A for the fast trains, and locals did not often use it. B and C were the normal departure platforms for the Glossop and Hadfield trains, and here of course they had to take turns with other locals working to Macclesfield, Marple and Hayfield. Platform B was separated from Platform A by a considerable distance, with four roads in between: these comprised the two platform roads and two middle roads normally used for storage of stock to avoid over-frequent journeys to the

carriage sidings at Ardwick. By contrast, there was only a single road between Platforms B and C serving both platforms; the origin of this very curious arrangement is not known, but its most obvious consequence was that, although trains leaving Platform C were always duly labelled as such on the train indicator boards, they were equally accessible from Platform B. The doors on the Platform B side had to be unlocked because they were in use at all subsequent stations. The only advantage of the arrangement was that passengers arriving in crowded morning local could detrain at either side, thus reducing congestion, though since everyone had to go through the same two barriers regardless of where they got out the difference was not very great. A decided disadvantage was that passengers who had arranged to meet on a train leaving Platform C often missed each other as a result of looking out of opposite sides of the train.

The first of the evening trains to Glossop though too early for most city workers, was the 4.35pm. It was a Gorton working throughout the time covered by this chapter, and worked direct into Glossop with the engine then proceeding bunker-first to Hadfield. It conveyed the evening newspapers – *Manchester Evening News* and *Evening Chronicle* in those days – to stations en route, and the need to unload these bulky parcels at Glossop may have been the reason it was allowed an extra minute's turn-round time. It was always awaited on the Glossop platform by a group of newsagents and their attendant newsboys, who swooped to tear open the parcels and stuff the contents into large delivery bags; because of this activity the 4.35 was often known in the town as the 'Paper Train'. Arrival at Glossop was 5.15 and after its call at Hadfield the train ran direct through Dinting to reach London Road again at 6.27pm, the engine being in time to work another commuters' train to Hayfield at 6.50.

The next evening departure for Glossop was something considerably out of the ordinary. By far the fastest train available to homecoming Glossopians, it can in fact go down in history as the fastest of all time, its time of 26 minutes remaining unsurpassed by the electrics of BR days: this was the famous 5.17, sometimes known for obvious reasons as the 'Glossop Express'. It achieved its remarkable time only by the somewhat unspectacular method of missing out stations, being 'first stop Broadbottom' in platform staff parlance, but of course its rapid schedule was immensely appreciated by those lucky enough to finish work in time to catch it. To Dinting Loco fell the honour of working this train, with the engine which had begun its day on the 6.50am from Hadfield, though now of course in different hands. Up to the summer of 1930 the 5.17 could not even e used by Dinting passengers, as it was most unusually booked non-stop from Broadbottom into Glossop – probably the only train ever to do this in normal service. However, in September 1930 a one-minute call at Dinting was introduced, and by slightly speeding up the non-stop run from London Road to Broadbottom it was possible to keep the Glossop arrival time of 5.43. The 5.17 was also unusual in not continuing on to Hadfield, for having discharged its passengers the stock was worked straight back to Dinting to connect with a following train due at 5.59.

This was none other than the 5.20pm for Hadfield, which less than three-quarters of an hour earlier had stood side by side with the 5.17 in London Road, one train at Platform B and the other in C. Never was the discrimination against Hadfield passengers more apparent than in the timing of these two trains, leaving Manchester so close together yet so different in schedule. Booked non-stop through Ardwick, Ashburys and Gorton, the 5.20 was far from being the slowest Hadfield train out of London Road, but by comparison with the 5.17 it seemed deadly slow, and for any unlucky Glossop passenger who chanced to miss the latter a journey on the 5.20 was like a prison sentence; the time-consuming change of trains at Dinting made for an eventual arrival in Glossop at 6.03, when most of those on the earlier train were already settling down comfortably at home, and the fact that one travelled from Dinting in the very same coaches added a further touch of indignity. The 5.20 was a Gorton working, and the engine and train returned from Hadfield as the 6.40 departure, which ran via Glossop; normally this was not a well-patronised train, and its main purpose was probably to get the engine and coaches quickly back into Manchester.

The next departure for Glossop was at 5.55pm, and on normal working days this was a very crowded train; it formed the return working of the third Dinting engine which had gone into Manchester with the 4.42 out of Glossop. It worked direct to Hadfield in the same way as the 5.20, passengers for Glossop changing once again into the stock of the erstwhile 5.17, now making its second trip along the branch. After a 25-minute turn-round at Hadfield the engine and stock worked into Glossop for 7.05, the coaches then being propelled into the Howard Street siding for the night, to become the branch train of next day. The 'F1' then retired to Dinting after putting in a single eight-hour shift.

To clear the platform for the 7.05 arrival from Hadfield, the stock of the 5.17 made yet another trip to Dinting at 6.40 to connect with the next arrival at 7.06. This was the 6.31 from London Road, well filled with Glossop passengers but in other respects very different from the rest of the

local services as it was a through train to Sheffield, formed of the stock of the 12.15pm Marylebone-Manchester express which had reached London Road at 5.15. Suburban travellers thus had a rare opportunity of sampling the very best main-line corridor stock, invariably in immaculate condition and complete with roofboards; the restaurant car was also open, so that it was possible to have one's evening meal on the way home from work, provided one could eat it in time. The purpose of this return stock working was to get the coaches into Sheffield where they could be prepared for the next morning's 7.30 Sheffield-Marylebone breakfast car express, forerunner of the postwar 'Master Cutler'. A Gorton engine was in charge of the 6.31pm, usually a 'B7' or 'J39', and of course this also gave the train a certain touch of distinction when compared with the usual 'F1' tanks.

For those late workers not able to make the 6.31pm the next available train was the recently introduced 6.45, which operated on a somewhat similar schedule to the 5.20, connecting at Dinting in the same way as the latter. A drawback of this train was the very long delay at Dinting, the branch connection waiting over a quarter of an hour before setting off to arrive in Glossop at 7.34, 16 minutes after the main train had reached Hadfield. The reason for this unusual timing is not known. The engine and stock left Hadfield at 7.42 and worked directly back into Manchester without calling at Glossop, the branch train once again furnishing a connection at Dinting. The 6.45 appears to have been something of an experiment because it did not survive in the timetable for very long, and during its brief currency alterations were made to the schedule of the return train from Hadfield. On its withdrawal at the beginning of September 1931 it was replaced by a similar train leaving at 7.10, which in fact was a reversion to the pre-1930 timetable. This worked direct to Hadfield and returned to London Road at 8.08, working via Glossop.

As far as the Dinting engine diagrams are concerned, it will have become apparent from what has been said that the engine of the 5.17 working eked out the rest of its day in a fairly leisurely manner by working trips to Dinting and back. There were five of these altogether, all connecting with main-line locals, and the last of them was completed with an arrival in Glossop at 9.14; the stock was then shunted into the goods warehouse road for the night and the engine retired to Dinting Loco to complete what must have been a fairly popular shift. The remaining Dinting engine, which had begun its had working the 7.10am trip to Dinting, was not involved with the evening rush trains to Glossop; instead it worked a local to Stalybridge and back and then acted as pilot at London Road until 9.40, when it worked a train to Hadfield. This was booked to call at all stations except Ardwick, and included a call at Glossop. After discharging the stock was shunted into the sidings to form the 6.50 of next morning, and the engine was released for Dinting Loco at about 10.45.

During the hours of darkness the small shed at Dinting became a hive of activity as the men of the night-shift set to work to give their engines the usual attentions – coaling, watering, examining, cleaning, and so on. The small staff of cleaners were expected to give the passenger engines a suitably thorough polishing, and in addition these energetic individuals were responsible for 'knocking up' – rousing the crews rostered for next morning's early turn. This entailed walking to their homes in various parts of Glossop and banging on the front door until some response was obtained from within; not surprisingly these nocturnal excursions sometimes led to eerie stories being told. Cleaners known to have been working at Dinting at about the time this chapter begins included Harry Isaacs, Bert Turner and Bill Ward.

In the 1930s working conditions differed from those of later years not only in longer daily hours, but also at weekends, when virtually everyone worked a half day on Saturday mornings, usually finishing between noon and one o'clock. Thus Saturday suburban services all over Britain followed much the same pattern, starting off as on normal weekdays and then altering in the late morning to provide a rush service lasting approximately from noon until about 1.30. The four trains serving Glossop and Hadfield during the midday peak were all Saturdays Only services, hence not to be found in the timetables on any other days.

First to leave was the 12.07pm, which ran direct to Hadfield without any connection for Glossop; this was rather early for a workers' train, and even those Glossop passengers who could get to London Road in time to catch it would probably not have done so, as the next train was into Dinting only six minutes later. This second train was the Saturday equivalent of the 5.17, leaving at 12.29pm to run non-stop to Broadbottom and then working directly into Glossop for 12.55. Somewhat unusually, this train proceeded straight back into Manchester after the five-minute reversal, and was easily the fastest of all the round trips between Manchester and Glossop. It and the 12.07 were Gorton turns, while the two later lunchtime trains were worked by Dinting. Of these the 12.48 also bore a certain resemblance to the 5.17, for although considerably slower it terminated at

Glossop in the same way, and the engine and stock were then diagrammed to spend the entire afternoon working connecting trips to and from Dinting, just as the 5.17 set did in the evenings and finished at 7.30pm without having made any further trips to Manchester. The 1.25 was a through Hadfield train via Glossop, after which the engine and stock worked back into Manchester again, leaving Hadfield at 3.40, and did not return again until the late evening when it formed the 9.40 from London Road to Hadfield, after which the engine went to Dinting.

In the opposite direction, Glossopians had the choice of four trains into Manchester, these being patronised mainly by shoppers and those attending sporting events, especially the ever-popular football. The best train was the 1pm departure already mentioned, which reached London Road in under half an hour, and for most of the football season allowed ample time to reach either of the League football grounds at Maine Road and Old Trafford, though not throughout, as in the day before floodlighting the longer nights meant earlier kick-offs during part of the season. There was a train into Manchester at 12.18 but this was too early for most people in Glossop and district. The two later trains, leaving Glossop at 1.34 and 2.30, were more popular with shoppers, the former being the return working of the 12.07 to Hadfield. The 2.30 was somewhat different, involving changing at Dinting into a Cleethorpes-Manchester express usually headed by one of Gorton's crack 'Directors'; the times were not very exciting, but for railway minded passengers there was a lot to be said for riding behind a spotless 'D11' with a Gorton Top Link crew on the footplate.

This Cleethorpes-Manchester service was one of the comparatively few main-line expresses which called at Dinting, the only other ones in that direction being a morning Cleethorpes booked to arrive at 11.46, and the 12.15pm Marylebone-Manchester express which made a lightning one-minute stop at 4.54. All three connections operated throughout the week as well as on Saturdays. In the up direction it was a rather different story, as although there were three expresses calling during the week, two of these the 12.40 to Cleethorpes and the 10.30pm Marylebone mail, omitted the Dinting stop on Saturdays because of the desire to avoid congestion on what were often very crowded weekend trains. This left only the 9.25am Hull express operating as an all-week train, but its morning call at Dinting (9.59) was clearly more for the benefit of those comparatively few passengers going in the Sheffield direction.

On certain down trains Dinting enjoyed the status of a request stop, but in these cases the passenger was dumped unceremoniously on the platform without any advertised connection for Glossop, while in the reverse direction one had to travel to Guide Bridge in order to catch the London or Hull expresses. In these circumstances it is hardly surprising that most Glossop passengers bound for London preferred to travel into Manchester and made use of the considerably quicker and more frequent trains to Euston.

The Saturday evening service into Glossop was similar to that operating during the week, except that the 5.17 and 5.55 did not run. At varying periods of time the 4.35pm was booked to terminate at Godley, where it attached the rear portion of the 2.50pm express from Hull and returned to London Road for 5.57; at other times it went through to Glossop as usual, omitted its weekday call at Hadfield and returned to Godley in time to connect with the Hull train as described. Its departure from Glossop at 5.20pm was preceded by a similar train at 5.10, and there were others at 5.48, 6.25, 7.39 and 8pm to cater for those wishing to sample the pleasures of the city, Manchester naturally being a popular venue for all types of entertainment; in addition there was also Belle Vue, which drew huge crowds to such diversions as boxing, wrestling, speedway and greyhounds, or to enjoy the large fun-fair. Passengers for Belle Vue detrained at Ashburys, which was always noted for being considerably busier on Saturdays than during the week. In the late evening three extra trains were provided to boost the normal departure at 9.40, leaving London Road at 9pm, 10.10 and 11.05, all for the benefit of the returning throng. The last of these trains usually conveyed more than its fair share of those who had been somewhat too liberal in their enjoyment, and the burdens of the long-suffering platform staff at stations en route were not infrequently added to by the need to assist such individuals out of the train and safely off the premises; occasionally differences of opinion arose, resulting in the intervention of officers of the law, and perhaps appearances in front of the local magistrates on the following Monday. Having discharged its passengers in Hadfield at 11.55, the train returned empty to Glossop and was placed in the Howard Street siding, to remain throughout Sunday and become the 7.35am to Manchester on Monday. This late train was worked by the Glossop goods pilot, which had gone into Manchester earlier in the evening, probably on the 8pm departure in the summer of 1930 and then from September on a new train leaving Glossop at 6pm; no doubt it was a very unpopular working as the crew would not get home until well after midnight, having spent most of the evening carriage shunting or doing similar menial jobs at London Road or Ardwick. The other late Saturday shift worked by Dinting terminated on the 9.40 departure from London Road, the stock being left in Hadfield at 10.30 for the weekend to become the Monday morning departure.

The last Saturday train out of Glossop left at 10.56, being the return of the 10.10 from London Road; this working formed the conclusion of a Gorton diagram which began at 5.40am and finished after midnight when the empty stock of the 10.56 was deposited at Ardwick, the engine having gone through the hands of three separate crews in the meantime. The 10.56 was another favourite amongst the pleasure-seeking fraternity, mainly because of differences in the licensing laws operative in the Glossop district; local public houses enjoyed the advantages of a later closing-time and were also licensed for music and singing, which was not the case in certain neighbouring towns. Visitors made particular use of these amenities during the summer, and one can imagine that on a typical Saturday evening in July or August the Glossop staff were not sorry to see the tail-light of the 10.56 disappearing in the distance.

The Sunday workings at Glossop were of an entirely different cast altogether, and surprisingly enough the Sabbath was from an observer's point of view probably the most interesting day of all. The reason was that most of the trains were not true locals in the proper sense of the word, but were really main-line trains routed along the branch to make a call at Glossop. In addition there were often unusual rostering developments on Sundays because of engines being in shed for maintenance, particularly at Gorton where engines newly repaired in the works often added to the variety. These circumstances could produce some quite unusual appearances on the Glossop line, ranging from 'Pom-Poms' to the very largest express passenger engines. The absence of the usual 'tankies' was accounted for by the fact that Sunday was their 'shed day'.

The first two arrivals at Glossop were typical of the Sunday pattern. The 6.40am out of London Road was a through stopping train to Sheffield, but unlike its weekday counterparts it travelled via Glossop, arriving at 7.28am. In the reverse direction came the 6.38 from Sheffield, reaching Glossop at 8.03 and continuing to Manchester after a rather leisurely eight-minute turn-round. Both trains were usually worked by tender engines, the former by a 'B7' or sometimes a 'B9', the latter probably by one of the 'D9s' which were so well represented at Neepsend Loco at that time. The Manchester-Sheffield train formed the beginning of a Gorton lodging turn that took the engine through to Immingham to return next day with an early morning goods. The arrival of larger engines at Glossop could always be distinguished in the vicinity of the station by a degree of vibration, and also by the more throaty exhaust; hence these early Sunday arrivals were not always popular with nearby residents. Probably the worst offenders were the occasional 'Pom-Poms', whose sharp beats echoed round the town like gunshots in the stillness of a Sabbath morning, while the disturbance was sometimes added to by violent blowing-off in the station since these Sunday workings were often in the care of less experienced crews.

Mixed goods and passenger diagrams of the kind just described were quite a feature of the Sunday workings, as there was a similar arrival at 9.53am on which the engine was going through to Sheffield to return next day as required, and at 4.19 in the afternoon, worked by an engine on its way to Immingham to return on a Monday fish job; this later became an Immingham turn and has been described in a previous volume[2]. In the opposite direction came the 12.20 from Sheffield, which was the return of a Gorton engine that had gone to Immingham on an Ashton-Moss-Grimsby goods early on Saturday morning; this however did not appear at Glossop, and instead the solitary Sunday branch working connected with it at Dinting at 1.40, getting back in Glossop at 1.54. The weekday branch workings were of course the exclusive province of Dinting Loco, but as they did not operate any passenger turns on Sundays this odd trip was most unusually fitted in as part of a Gorton suburban diagram.

During these years the town of Glossop could number a variety of churches and chapels amongst its institutions, most fairly well attended, and such a degree of Sabbath observance meant that the trains are not likely to have been particularly well-patronised: indeed it seems surprising that the service should have been as frequent as it was. It seems highly unlikely that any local person, churchgoer or otherwise, would have wished to travel either to Manchester or Sheffield before nine o'clock on a Sunday morning, and so for the few main-line passengers aboard these early trains the journey into and out of Glossop can only have been a tiresome detour. Some of the trains seem particularly ill-suited to local requirements, the most notable one being the 2.47pm arrival, which had started from, of all places, Oldham Clegg Street; it lingered in Glossop Central until 3.10 and then shuffled off back to Oldham again, reversing at Guide Bridge as on the outward trip. No weekday equivalent of this most unusual through service is known to have existed during LNER days, and it is difficult to believe that such a train could ever have been much patronised from either

end, yet it survived in the timetables until the outbreak of war. It must go down to posterity as the outstanding curio of the Glossop local service.

The most dedicated patrons of the Sunday services came from among the ranks of the walking fraternity, known in those days as 'hikers' and usually hailing from the Manchester area. Hiking was a pastime that increased enormously in popularity in the years between the wars, and it was much encouraged by the railway companies as a useful addition to revenue; many booklets and pamphlets have survived to testify to this, a great many published by the LNER, and the importance of Glossop in this connection was that it gave ready access to the well-known Derbyshire Peakland, as well as the Cheshire moors in the vicinity of Woodhead and Greenfield. The walking season traditionally began on Good Friday, and on that day extra locals referred to as 'hikers' specials' were usually put on, while during the spring and summer the Glossop service was augmented by an extra train in each direction, the outward one usually leaving some time after 11am, with a return about 7.30pm; these were diagrammed as part of the same turn, which also included the Glossop branch trip referred to earlier.

Another feature of the Sunday service, resulting from the diversion into Glossop of main-line stopping trains as already described, was the much wider use of bogie stock instead of the six-wheelers that reigned on weekdays, and it was therefore ironic that this unaccustomed comfort should have been made comparatively little use of by local travellers. The Manchester suburban service as a whole was characterised by the very small number of local stock workings on Sundays, and on that day most of the numerous sets were to be found congregated in the sidings at Ardwick, which gave most of workforce a well-earned day off while a small staff attended to such cleaning and routine repair work as was necessary.

Platform hands at Glossop Central did not look forward to Sunday with quite the same enthusiasm as the Ardwick staff, as although there were no morning and evening rush-hours to worry about, the day brought its own tribulations. One of them was the shorter shift worked by the booking office staff, which meant that at the start and finish of the day more time had to be spent issuing tickets, a task which most platform staff heartily disliked; the nuisance was at its worst when local excursions were being run, as no matter how late the arrival of the return train, a member of the platform staff had to be on hand to collect tickets prior to locking up. The local Wakes Week was the worst time for this, as specials were frequently booked to arrive back after midnight and were often late. Another annoyance associated with late-evening manning of the booking-office was that all money taken had be balanced and sales of tickets accounted for; cash discrepancies had to be notified, though the staff were no doubt grateful for the fact that they were not expected to make good any deficiencies from their own pocket!

Yet another Sunday headache arose from the use of large engines. Measuring 63ft over buffers, a B7' 4-6-0 could only just be accommodated in the reversing spur at the end of the platform, and in the hands of a driver not used to the local service could prove difficult to position correctly without striking the buffer-stops; time spent in this manoeuvre often led to delay and resulted in the circulation of one of the hated explanation forms, requiring someone to 'carry the can'. A redeeming feature was that, as a result of the history of frequent Sunday delays, the turn-round times on most trains had been eased out a little by 1930.

Sunday evening at Glossop finished off in typical style with the arrival at 9.09 of yet another engine involved in one of the mixed goods and passenger diagrams. This had gone through to Cleethorpes on an early morning parcels train from London Road, and after lodging at Immingham during the day the crew set off back on a passenger train due out of Cleethorpes at 4.30pm and worked right through to Manchester. Their arrival in Glossop on the footplate of a main-line engine, leading in a rake of bogie stock, could hardly have been more characteristic of the Sunday scene in that part of the world, and even the platform staff could take comfort from the fact that it was allowed a comfortable nine minutes in which to turn round.

The most important development affecting the Glossop services after 1930 was the introduction of push-and-pull working. Unfortunately it has not been possible to determine exactly when this took place, but it is believed to have been between the latter part of 1931 and the summer of 1932. It is known for certain that it was in operation by September 1932, and the fact that an 'F1' engine, No 5729, was fitted with the special push-and-pull gear at Gorton in the previous November is thought to have some bearing on the matter. The special control gear carried by push-and-pull fitted engines enabled them to be attached more or less permanently to a coach or coaches provided with a driving compartment, so that the train could then be operated from either end without the engine switching round; when running coach-first the driver occupied the special compartment at what now became the front of the train, while the fireman remained aboard the engine. The driving compartment was fitted with brake, regulator and whistle control, and communication between the two members of the crew was made possible by a bell-code or by the use of the engine whistle.

Push-and-pull working offered many advantages, especially in the working of branch passenger services, and its history on the GCR goes back to before Grouping, but as far as is known it had never previously been tried in the Glossop area. The decision to introduce it seems to have been part of a general expansion of push-and-pull working which the LNER put into effect from the early 1930s onwards, probably with the aim of securing greater economy in working.

The introduction of the push-and-pull at Dinting Loco resulted in a major reshuffle of the passenger workings, involving the complete disappearance of one of the diagrams and consequent reduction in the number of Class 'F1' engines stationed there. The two diagrams that remained were an amalgam of the previous workings, with the push-and-pull taking charge of all the branch trips – formerly worked by three different engines at various times, including the Glossop goods pilot as described earlier; the use of the push-and-pull on the branch trains was particularly desirable because of the elimination of running round the train at Dinting and Glossop stations, exactly the style of operation for which the motor trains had been developed. In addition to these, the push-and-pull worked a morning and an evening trip to Manchester, the former as the 7.35 from Glossop after a trip to Hadfield at 7.10, so that the 7.35 now became a through train from Hadfield instead of a purely Glossop departure as formerly; the evening diagram involved departure from Glossop with the lightly-patronised 4.42 and then a return from Manchester as the high-speed 5.17. The morning and evening commuters' trains were of course much too crowded for the push-and-pull to accommodate all the passengers in its modest two coaches, one of them a six-wheeler, and so for these workings extra stock was attached; for the 7.35am the motor train ran coaches-first into the Howard Street siding on its return from Hadfield and coupled up to the set of stock which had been stored there from the previous day's workings; a substantial train was thus formed, and after arrival at London Road the extra coaches were detached to be used elsewhere. In the evening the push-and-pull arrived coaches-first in London Road and was immediately attached to a set of stock waiting at the platform to form the 5.17; on arrival at Glossop the extra coaches were promptly detached and drawn out by the goods pilot so that the motor train was free to work directly back to Dinting to connect with the 5.20 from London Road. The spare coaches remained at Glossop during the evening, and late at night were worked empty to Ardwick carriage sidings for their next day's working.

To enable the push-and-pull to attach its extra

coaches in the morning and evening it had to be worked facing opposite directions at different times of the day. In the mornings it left Dinting Loco with the engine facing Manchester, and duly performed the 7.35 working with the engine at the front in the normal way; returning from Manchester as empty stock at 8.30, it ran round the triangle at Dinting station and arrived in Glossop at 9.07am engine-first; it then remained with the engine facing east throughout the rest of its day. However, because of the position of the coaling-stage at Dinting Loco it was impossible to coal the engine in this direction, and so on its departure from Glossop at the end of the day it once again went via the triangle at Dinting so that the engine could be coaled, and the train was now facing the right way for its working the next morning.

The introduction of the push-and-pull set a new standard as far as comfort was concerned, for the rear vehicle of the two-coach set was a 12-wheel open third which gave a remarkably smooth ride, and the large picture windows offered a much enhanced view; the roomy interior was also a big improvement on the cramped compartments of the contemporary six-wheelers, and so the coach became a great favourite with regular travellers.

The push-and-pull working did not survive for very long in the form just described, though the reasons for the change can only be surmised. In all probability it was felt that the engine and coaches were considerably under-utilised on the 13 branch trips which formed the bulk of their daily duty, for in many cases the coaches ran empty and in addition a great deal of time was spent standing at the platform at Glossop Central. Early in September 1933 a number of new trains to Manchester made their appearance in the local timetable, among which the 12.12 and 2.02 were diagrammed for the push-and-pull, with return trains from London Road at 1pm and 2.45pm. Forming two complete round trips, these extra workings swelled the number of daily journeys to Manchester to four as against the original two, and it is believed that the train continued to operate in this form until the outbreak of war brought changes in the timetable. Now that it was fully employed during the afternoon on trips to Manchester, the push-and-pull was no longer able to officiate as branch train during that part of the day, and so the faithful goods pilot was once again commandeered for passenger duty, working three trips to Dinting and back between 12.50 and 3.25pm; during this period of the day therefore the branch train now consisted of two coaches based permanently at Glossop for the purpose, headed by a 'Pom-Pom'.

The introduction of the extra push-and-pull trips to Manchester saw the appointment of a porter-guard from among the ranks of the Glossop platform staff, his responsibility being to officiate as guard on the two afternoon Manchester workings, in addition to his normal platform duties during the rest of the shift. Alf Swindells was the name of the man chosen, and because of his additional work as a guard he worked the same shift each week.

Modernisation overtook the Glossop services very gradually during these years, and it was not until about 1935 that the first change-over from six-wheel to bogie stock was made. The larger vehicles were not of course new, having been simply transferred from other parts of the LNER when displaced by still newer carriage stock; some are believed to have come from the Marylebone services. Their use on the Glossop trains saw the gradual disappearance of the old gaslit six-wheelers, for so long familiar in the district, and probably as unpopular with the railway staff as they were with the public, particularly in the winter when the tiresome chore of putting on the gas lights had to be performed twice daily. The bogie vehicles were of course electrically lit, and their more sophisticated suspension gave a very much smoother ride; thanks to such refinements, the Glossop passengers could now compare themselves reasonably favourably with those suburban travellers using the adjacent LMS platforms at London Road. The worn-out six-wheel coaches went for scrap, but it is interesting that one of them was retained by the Engineers' Department and was parked permanently on the down side of Dinting Arches, overlooking Adderley Place, for use as a tool store; here it remained, its original blue paint gradually fading to a weatherbeaten grey, until long after World War 2.

No exact date for replacement of the six-wheel stock can be given, but the push-and-pull was photographed working with a bogie coach in September 1938[3], and this is thought to have replaced the previous six-wheeler a short time before.

By the time the bogie stock came on the scene the now very elderly 'F1' tanks were beginning to be withdrawn, the first one having departed as early as 1930. Besides, the 2-4-2s were beginning to find the heavier bogie stock something of a trial on some of the busier morning and evening workings, and these developments led to the introduction of another class of tank engine that was to have a long association with the Glossop services, the 'C13' 4-4-2s. No 5002, the first to be transferred to Gorton, arrived in November 1934, followed by No 5115 in the succeeding January, and further members of the class continued to arrive up to and beyond the outbreak of war. They were destined eventually to take over the whole of the Glossop service, but this stage had not been reached at September 1939, when there were still a small number of 'F1s' in service at Gorton.

Another class which also came on the scene in the mid-1930s were the 'F2' tanks, outwardly very similar to the older 'F1s'; they had been associated with the Liverpool suburban workings for many years, but were gradually transferred to Gorton from 1933 onwards, and took a share in the Glossop service. After several of them had been fitted with an improved type of push-and-pull gear in 1936-37 they took over the motor train services operated from Gorton, including of course the Glossop push-and-pull. The engines involved were Nos 5776, 5777 and 5782 replacing 'F1s' 5575, 5586 and 5729, and the switch-over is known to have been completed by the autumn of 1937, although it has been recorded [4] that another 'F1', No 5594, which had performed for a number of years in the Neasden district working the Quainton Road-Verney Junction push-and-pull, was retained in motor-fitted condition at Gorton to act as a spare for the regular push-and-pull engines.

Owing to the unfortunate lack of observers' notes it has proved impossible to discover exactly when the Class C13 and F2 engines first appeared on the Glossop trains, but in the case of the former it is fairly certain that they were kept to specific diagrams, operated exclusively from the parent depot instead of being outstationed at Dinting. By the time they began to establish themselves on the scene there had in any case been a further reduction in the passenger work performed at Dinting Loco, for the summer of 1937 saw only one daily passenger diagram being operated from the sub-shed instead of the previous two. This last surviving diagram involved the Glossop push-and-pull itself, which with its early and late shifts required only two sets of passenger men.

The cutting down of work at Dinting resulted in the transfer of men to the main shed at Gorton, and was part of a process whereby the sub-shed was eventually closed completely in the following year, with all crews now based at Gorton and all turns diagrammed to start and finish there. A similar fate had already overtaken the two other sub-sheds at Hayfield and Macclesfield, and no doubt the aim behind these developments, as the reader may well guess, was economy. The move naturally led to a migration of Dinting staff into Manchester because of the travelling which residence in the Glossop district now entailed, though it should be borne in mind that as Dinting men progressed through the various grades they invariably had to spend a certain time at Gorton as there was insufficient work at the subshed; there

were even some who had gone to Gorton and never come back, the best-known of these probably being Joe Chamberlain, who after transferring from Dinting in GCR days eventually rose to become Trial Trip driver in succession to Jack Howard.

With all suburban locomotives now based at Gorton it was necessary for light engine working to take place at the beginning and end of each day in order to operate the Glossop services, the expense of such unprofitable running evidently being well offset by the economies achieved in closing Dinting Loco.

It has already been said in this chapter that observers' notes of the Glossop scene have been hard to come by, and even visits to Dinting shed appear to have been rare occurrences. The earliest notes that have been traced refer to Saturday 2 September 1933, when an observer at Dinting station saw 'F1s' Nos 5574 and 5577 during the afternoon, no doubt working on Glossop and Hadfield locals. A visit to Dinting Loco on Sunday 25 November 1934 revealed 'F1s' Nos 5579 and 5586, the latter motor-fitted and evidently the current Glossop push-and-pull engine. A photograph taken on Sunday 24 February 1935 shows 'F1' No 5575 attached to the push-and-pull carriage set, standing alongside the shed building at Dinting Loco with the engine recently coaled and correctly facing west, in readiness for its Monday morning duties.

A glimpse of how the less numerous 'C13' tanks were diagrammed can be seen in notes taken at Godley station on Saturday 4 June 1938, when No 5457, sent to Gorton in February of the previous year, was observed making two round trips to Glossop and Hadfield during the middle of the day; seen returning from Hadfield on the 10.55am after having worked the 10.05 out of London Road, it went to Glossop again with the 12.27 and came back on the 1.01 Glossop-Manchester. The second out-and-back working has already been described as the smartest out-and-back working between Manchester and Glossop, and with six well-filled bogie coaches, as on the day in question, it forms a typical example of the kind of work which was being regularly done by the more powerful 'C13' engines. Other rather less usual appearances on the Glossop locals that day included 'J39' No 1290 of Retford on what was probably the 12.48pm Manchester-Glossop and return working at 2.25pm after depositing some coaches at the latter, 'J11s' Nos 5254 and 6045 on evening trains, and 'C4' Atlantic No 5266 of Lincoln, recently repaired at Gorton Works and evidently running in on the 4.35pm to Glossop; perhaps the gem of them all was Gorton's No 5503 *Somme* working what was probably the 12.07pm to Hadfield and duly returning on the 1.32

53

Hadfield-Manchester. This and the 'J39' were evidently being used on fill-in trips to Glossop prior to main-line workings, as No 1290 later set off on its long trek home to Retford with the 3.52pm Manchester-Sheffield stopping train, while No 5503 *Somme* turned up on the 5pm Cleethorpes express out of Manchester. Such locomotive variety was perhaps more typical of the Glossop service on Sundays, but it is perhaps significant that the day in question was the Saturday preceding Whit Sunday, the beginning of one of the most popular holiday periods in the Manchester area in those days. A not dissimilar mixture was noted during the afternoon of Saturday 10 June in the following year, with 'K3' No 3816 doing one of the Glossop round trips, 'N5' No 5928 putting in an appearance, and then a touch of startling modernity supplied by 'V2' No 4828 working the 6.31pm to Sheffield – traditionally a 'big engine' turn. 'Pom-Poms' Nos 5327 and 6004 were also on the scene, the former doing two trips of which the second involved the 7.10pm direct to Hadfield and return on the 8.04 via Glossop. No 6004 is believed to have been noted on the 6.05pm ex-Glossop which for some years was regularly diagrammed for the Glossop goods pilot, working into Manchester with stock left from the 12.48pm earlier in the day, and returning on the 11.05pm from London Road; this applies also to 'J11' No 6045 quoted in the notes for June 1938.

The 1939 date given above was a normal Saturday, and such appearances suggest that the intensive pattern of tank engine workings that was such a feature of the ordinary weekdays was somewhat disrupted on Saturday afternoons, and that it was becoming the custom of the Gorton running foremen to turn out whatever engine happened to be lying handy when it came to filling a gap in the Glossop workings. It is likely also that the closure of Dinting shed had had some effect on this situation.

Details from the various notes quoted above indicate that by the late 1930s the Glossop local trains were usually made up to six or seven bogie coaches at busy times, and about four during off-peak periods. The hardy six-wheelers had not entirely disappeared from the scene in June 1938, as two of the trains were noted as consisting of these distinctive vehicles, one of them drawn by the immaculate 'C4' No 5266 already referred to. The 1939 notes contain no reference to six-wheeled stock, and the conjunction of these two dates can be taken as a rough guide to the time of their final demise.

So far as concerns the identities of the various men who worked the Glossop services during these years, the reader will already be aware that the work was largely divided between Gorton and Dinting sheds, until the closure of the latter in 1938. At Gorton there was a regular suburban link covering workings to Glossop, Macclesfield, Hayfield and Stalybridge, and because of the popularity of such work there were a number of men who chose to remain in the link for many years, and who probably finished their time there; they included J. Avison, E. Birchenall, G. Clark, F. Hadfield, J. Knowles, J. Poyser, A. Redman, J. W. Stanley and F. Williamson. To these men fell the task of working some of the best suburban turns out of London Road, and among other things they were probably the first footplatemen to drive the 'C13' tanks when they arrived at Gorton from 1934.

As for the Glossop end of the service, a convenient guide to the local personnel is given in the list of mourners attending the funeral of former driver Jimmy Ryan, who passed away on 22 April 1931 after nearly 50 years of railway service during which 'for a long period he had been an engine-driver on the Glossop Branch', as the local newspaper has it. In 1930 Driver Ryan was one of the senior drivers at Dinting Loco, and prominent among the mourners was his colleague of almost exactly the same seniority, Jimmy Reid; other top-ranking footplatemen who attended were Joe Parker, Alf Booth, John Tommy Bramwell and Bill Hadfield, while further down the seniority scale were Ernie Gray and Bob Boak, the latter a sometime Mayor of Glossop and destined to be running foreman at Dinting shed when it reopened during the war. Younger hands present at the funeral were Bill Hague, Bill Norbury and Percy Heppenstall, all in the firing grades at this time. To complete a broad railway representation, the mourners included George Denham, shunter at Glossop, and Bob Hewitt, who when not on duty as signalman in Glossop box was usually to be found officiating as master of ceremonies at the local dance-hall.

Other senior footplate staff unable to attend the funeral included Bill Isaacs, Bill Parker and Albert Goodwin. By 1936 these and several of those named above had retired, and the four passenger drivers at Dinting were Alf Mansfield, Walter Oldham, Harry Lewis and Alf Booth. Driver Mansfield had had an interesting career in that he had transferred from Neasden to Dinting as driver of the unique petrol-electric car about 1914, and chose to remain at Dinting after the car moved on to Macclesfield shortly before Grouping. His regular fireman was Jimmy Farrell, and the other three passenger firemen were Bill Hague, Stanley Bevan and Bill Norbury, though it is not known ith which drivers they were teamed. Besides knowing the Glossop-Manchester line, the Dinting crews also worked turns to Stalybridge and Marple.

Passenger guards came from Manchester London Road, Glossop and Hadfield, but the only names which have been traced are John Barratt and Herman Fox, the latter retiring in April 1933; they were based at Glossop and Hadfield respectively. One of the Glossop guards is recalled as having been responsible for the job of ordering supplies of chocolate for the slot-machines on the platform, receiving a small commission on sales.

Besides Bob Hewitt, local signalmen included Charlie Carter, who spent many years in Dinting station box, Jimmy Walsh and Jack Whitehead who worked in the box at Hadfield station, Bill Bradley who was for a long time relief signalman in the district, and the brothers Billy and Tommy Doyle.

Accidents involving the Glossop local trains seem to have been unknown during the years covered by this chapter, but there was one sad incident which occurred in the early morning of 14 October 1935 as the 6.50 Hadfield-Manchester train was negotiating Hattersley cutting, between Broadbottom and Godley stations. Looking through the spectacle glass, Driver Walter Oldham saw the figure of a woman standing near to the lineside, but although he blew his whistle in warning she did not move away; then as the train came within a short distance she suddenly lay down on the line, and although Driver Oldham made a prompt application of the brakes he was unable to stop in time. A verdict of suicide was returned on the woman, who was a resident of Godley.

As with so much else that is described in this book, the war brought great changes to the Glossop service, and by the time hostilities ended it was scarcely recognisable from prewar days, not only because of changes in the timetable but also because of the complete replacement of the long-serving 2-4-2 tanks by Class C13 engines. In any event however, the service as it has been described in this chapter was doomed to disappear once electrification of the line had been carried out, work on which had already commenced before the war started. Hence the Glossop and Hadfield service of the 1930s was really no more than a final interlude in the transition from steam to electric haulage, and thus already belonged to a bygone age.

Notes
1 Jackson & Russell, *The Great Central in LNER Days*, Chapter 12.
2 Jackson & Russell, *The Great Central in LNER Days*, Chapter 12.
3 RCTS, *Locomotives of the LNER, Part 7*, frontispiece.
4 **RCTS, *Locomotives of the LNER, Part 7*.**

Below:
Dinting Arches in pre-Grouping days, before the extra brick piers were built. A train of typical six-wheelers approaches Dinting station with a tank engine in charge, running bunker-first. *H. Bowdur collection*

Top:
An 'F1' in early LNER guise. No 727 is at Gorton Loco, with the coaling stage in the background. *Real Photos*

Above:
A typical scene at Hayfield in 1926. 'J11' No 5327 stands near a rake of six-wheel coaches a short distance from the station. *W. Potter collection*

Top right:
Aerial view of Glossop taken on 8 April 1949, but largely unchanged from prewar days. *H. Bowdur collection*

Right:
Glossop station frontage on 5 April 1969.
H. Bowdur collection

Left:
'F2' No 5776 fitted with vacuum-operated push-and-pull gear as used on the Glossop service, pictured about 1937. *W. Leslie Good, per W. T. Stubbs*

Centre left:
'F1' No 5594 in push-and-pull service at Aylesbury in the early 1930s. The engine is fitted with the mechanically-controlled push-and-pull gear. The 12-wheel coach with central door is very similar to that used on the Glossop service. *Real Photos*

Bottom left:
'F2' No 7106 in push-and-pull service at Guide Bridge,

probably working the Oldham train. The engine was originally No 5778 but had been renumbered when this picture was taken about 1946. *Real Photos*

Below:
'C13' tanks began to appear on the Glossop and Hadfield services from the mid-1930s. No 5193 is outside the Gorton paintshop on 25 July 1937, following an overhaul. *Photo W. Leslie Good, per W. T. Stubbs*

Bottom:
A typical Sheffield suburban train of the interwar years. 'C13' No 6055 of Neepsend Loco enters Sheffield Victoria from the east on 14 September 1929. *Photo W. Leslie, per W. T. Stubbs*

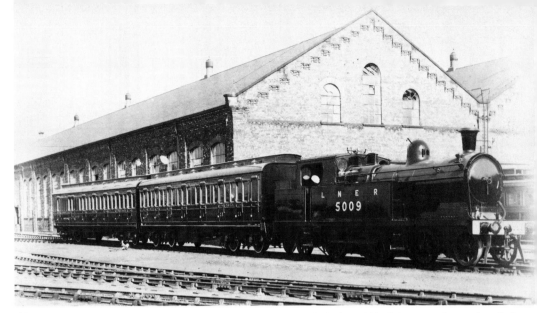

Above:
Newly painted 'C13' No 5009 is seen outside Dukinfield Carriage Works with two immaculate bogie coaches, Nos 5154 and 5407, in the mid-1930s. The engine has mechanical push-and-pull gear. *W. A. Brown collection*

Below:
'C13' No 5457 was a frequent performer on the Glossop
locals in the late 1930s. It is seen at Gorton Loco in June 1937.
Photo E. Neve

Bottom:
Tanks for the memory. An assortment of GCR types awaiting scrapping at Gorton Works on 21 August 1958.
Photo P. H. Groom

IV

Long Day in London

Extra Long Day in London. 16½ hours for 19s 4d. Easons' have arranged a specially long day excursion for Saturday 29 September. It will leave Grimsby about 4 am and arrive at Kings Cross about 7.30 am, giving 16½ hours in Town for 19s 4d, whilst cheap period bookings will also be given.

The *Grimsby News*,
Friday 14 September 1923

The special excursion traffic which operated between Cleethorpes and London Kings Cross was very much a feature of the period with which this book deals. Few of those who observed trains regularly on the GNR section lines between Grimsby, Peterborough and Kings Cross could have failed to notice the regular flow of trains from Cleethorpes, usually appearing on Thursdays and Saturdays; they stood out all the more because of the use of GCR locomotives in what was, particularly south of Peterborough, very much a Great Northern stronghold. It is because of this Great Central 'presence' that the story of the specials can claim a place in this book, for apart from a two-mile stretch between Cleethorpes and Grimsby the workings took place entirely on former GNR metals.

From a purely Great Central point of view the interest of the story is considerably enhanced by the fact that over the years the specials featured the use of no fewer than four different types of Gorton-designed 4-6-0s, some of them regarded as among the most handsome of John G. Robinson's products. Proof of their eye-catching qualities may be seen in what the *Grimsby News* had to say about a Class B3 engine currently stationed in the district: '*Early Beatty* is seen leaving Grimsby every day at 1 pm with the express for Leicester', it announced in its issue of 17 August 1923. 'It excites the admiration of everyone by its beautiful design and fine colouring.' One hopes that such laudatory remarks were brought to the attention of the Gorton Works staff, although by this time of course their esteemed chief was settling down to enjoy a well-earned retirement in faraway Bournemouth. Like most GCR 4-6-0s the 'B3s'

have so far been comparatively little noticed in railway literature, and so this chapter affords a very welcome opportunity to fill the gap a little in respect both of the 'B3s' and the other types used on the Cleethorpes-London specials.

The excursions of the period 1923-39 were of three main types, depending on the body responsible for organising them. Some were arranged by the LNER and advertised in the normal way on the company's notices and handbills; others were put on by Messrs Dean & Dawson, the well-known firm of travel agents which had operated in close concert with the MSLR and GCR from the previous century[1], and in the third category were those organised by a Grimsby-based travel agency known as Easons'. Of these three concerns it was the last-named which can claim to have started the fashion of running excursions from northeast Lincolnshire to London.

J. W. Eason, owner and founder of the Grimsby travel agents, was a notable example of a species often encountered in Victorian times – the self-made man. The son of a farm labourer in Spalding, he had started life in humble circumstances before migrating to Grimsby to become, in time, merchant, travel agent, proprietor of the *Grimsby News*, Justice of the Peace, and a leading Liberal on the local town council. A search for more attractive ways of building up his travel business had led him to consider the possibility of popularising day excursions to London, and in this he naturally turned to the GCR's local rival the Great Northern as it possessed by far the most direct route to the capital; no doubt his choice was also influenced by the presence of a Dean & Dawson office in Grimsby (on Cleethorpe Road, adjacent to the docks), as this meant that he was unable to act as a local agent for the Great Central. The Easons' Specials, as they soon became known, were operated entirely by the GNR therefore, being worked from Grimsby Town station to Kings Cross via the East Lincolnshire line through Louth, Boston, and Eason's birthplace at Spalding to reach the company's main line at Werrington Junction and so through to London. Beginning as early as 1905, the excursions were a success from the start and continued to operate as described right up to Grouping.

From an LNER point of view however the arrangements inherited in 1923 were in some respects less than satisfactory. The Great Northern had never possessed very much in the way of facilities at Grimsby, and to operate the excursions it was necessary for an engine and coaches to be sent there specially and then returned afterwards; as the engines and probably the stock came from Peterborough the arrangement involved a good deal of unproductive running. Clearly, far more efficient working could be achieved by transferring the workings to Immingham shed, only about five miles away from Grimsby Town. This meant of course that the turns would be taken over by the GCR, and no doubt it was a scheme which appealed strongly to the mind of the newly-appointed Loco Running Superintendent, W. G. P. Maclure. Likewise, coaches could be provided from the GC section sidings at Cleethorpes, thus eliminating the working of empty stock up and down the 78 miles between Peterborough and Grimsby.

The switch-over of working brought into existence a diagram bearing the characteristic GCR stamp, for the opportunity of creating a lucrative long-distance turn for the Immingham crews was not one that the new running superintendent would be likely to let slip. Under the new arrangements the GCR engine and men were booked to work right through to Kings Cross, instead of handing over to a GN section engine at either Boston or Peterborough, as could just as easily have been arranged. The new working of course involved lodging at Kings Cross, but to Great Central men such things were, almost literally, meat and drink. From the higher management's point of view such long-distance workings were in any event regarded as more economical – when the former GCR Superintendent W. Clow read a paper to the Institute of Transport in 1925 he stressed this very point when dealing with the question of more economic operation.

The switch to Great Central responsibility meant of course that the chosen crews had to learn the road through to Kings Cross; though the GNR line entered Grimsby at Garden Street Junction, just a few yards from Town station, it was foreign territory to the GCR crews expect for a few drivers who had worked special trains over it during the Great War. Among these was Sid Cleaver, who had had the distinction of working troop trains over the Great Northern and so because of his existing knowledge of at least a part of the road he became a natural choice for the new working. A second driver, Bill Croft, was also taught the road, the original idea being that the two men should work alternate trips. These new long-distance workings were very much at the top of the tree as far as prestige was concerned, and Messrs Cleaver and Croft could probably have boasted, had they chosen to do so, that they were the

best-remunerated enginemen at Immingham i those days.

The excursions normally ran on Thursdays an Saturdays, an arrangement that had becom established in pre-Grouping days when th discerning J. W. Eason decided that they offere the best prospects for business: Saturday was much a favourite 'day out' then as it is now, an Thursday was half-day closing in Grimsby an district. During the summer season there wa usually an excursion every week, and in the wint months perhaps every fortnight or three week Departure time was normally around 7am an arrival at Kings Cross about 10.30, with man slight variations over the years. Return was usual at midnight or thereabouts, giving patrons a fu afternoon and evening in the capital.

The popularity of the trains was never in doub and the only change wrought by the passing years was a steady increase in custom. B Grouping, Eason's competitors were well aware the rosy prospects which the traffic offered, an

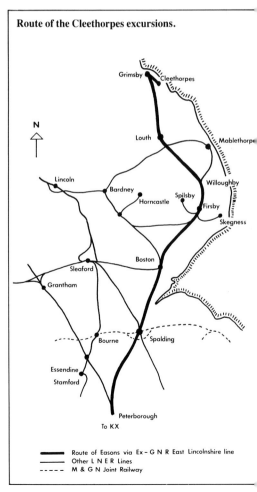

Route of the Cleethorpes excursions.

Route of Easons via Ex-G N R East Lincolnshire line
———— Other L N E R Lines
- - - - M & G N Joint Railway

e LNER were soon advertising their own xcursions to London, while Dean & Dawson's lso got into the act, although in the main it evoted itself to promoting foreign travel. At opular times half-day excursions were put on,)metimes organised by Eason's and sometimes by 1e LNER, usually booked to reach Kings Cross bout 2.30 in the afternoon. The flair and nterprise originally shown by J. W. Eason in re-World War 1 days had thus undoubtedly had a rofound effect on the travel habits of Grimsby eople, and so eventually on the fortunes of the NER. Sad to say, he did not live to see the ontinuing promotion of his original idea as he ied in November 1923.

A later generation of readers may perhaps find it ifficult to understand why the excursions were so opular. Those accustomed to more modern 1ethods of travel, and particularly to the virtues of 1e private car, may well find the idea of large umbers of people patronising railway outings to ondon somewhat curious, if not actually bizarre. rdinary people of the interwar years had a very ifferent outlook on life compared to that of more ecent generations, mainly because of lack of 1oney and the unavailability of cheap goods. The rivate car, vastly more expensive in relation to verage earnings than it has become in more ecent times, was an amenity that lay far beyond 1e reach of ordinary families. Yet in these years 1e amount of leisure time available to working eople, though limited by the standards of later ears, was nevertheless increasing, and with it 1ere was the desire to get about and see)mething of the world. London, as always, was a eat attraction: its history and famous buildings ew sightseers in increasing numbers, while the rge shops of Oxford Street and its vicinity were 1 additional attraction for the womenfolk. esides these things there was always a huge riety of cultural and sporting events to be mpled.

Another important factor in the travel business, 1d one that had been well understood by Eason, as that of personal comfort. His excursions fered guaranteed seats on all trains, and meals ere served in both directions. This constituted a ry different proposition from the usual excursion ains offered by the railway companies, formed 1t of whatever coaching stock happened to be ing handy, and often lacking even toilet facilities cause of the use of non-corridor stock. Among e staff who travelled with each train was the vner's son, known to one and all as 'Bunny' 1son; he attended to the passengers' comfort and so dealt with complaints.

The price, equalling 97p in present-day money, as not of course as low as it sounds to modern rs, but was within the budget of most ordinary

people provided they or some member of their family was in regular employment. Those who were a little better off might opt to stay in London, travelling up on the Thursday and returning on Saturday night, all for an inclusive price.

A factor which undoubtedly contributed to the growing popularity of the various London excursions over the years was the success achieved by the local Association Football Club, Grimsby Town. After being among the 'small fry' of the Football League at the time of Grouping, the team gained promotion to the Second Division in 1926, and reached the premier division three years after that. Though a relatively small club it was always extremely well supported, and had a devoted following who regularly travelled to away games. The rise into the upper reaches of the League meant that the team began to make regular visits to the well-known London clubs, notably Tottenham Hotspur, Chelsea, West Ham United and, above all, the mighty Arsenal. Excursions in connection with such games were invariably laid on, either by Eason's or the other agencies, and sometimes fixtures were arranged to fall at popular times – Grimsby Town often played in London, for instance, on Boxing Day. On many occasions therefore supporters and their families would travel to the match and enjoy the pleasures of the capital afterwards. It should perhaps be added that the general behaviour of football fans in those days was usually very different from what it has become in more recent times; unfavourable crowd reactions during matches were not uncommon, but were seldom serious enough to interfere with play, and away from the terraces most supporters were largely indistinguishable from ordinary members of the public. All the railway companies welcomed the extra revenue which the game generated, and in the case of the Cleethorpes trains there is little doubt that the habit of travelling to London helped to stimulate custom on non-sporting occasions.

It was not until several months after Grouping that the change-over to Great Central working actually took place, the Eason's and other excursions of early LNER days continuing to appear at Kings Cross behind Class C1 Atlantics from New England Loco. The first known appearance of a GCR engine is Saturday 29 September – the excursion referred to at the head of this chapter – and research suggests that this was almost certainly the first-ever Immingham working.

As to why the Loco Running Department should have waited so long before putting into effect what, as described earlier, was such an obvious improvement to the working arrange- ments, the answer lies probably in the large-scale reorganisation then taking place as the fledgling LNER set to work to gather together the various parts of its far-flung empire. Also there was inevitable time-lag in connection with new appointments, W. G. P. Maclure not being made Running Superintendent until April. No doubt also it was thought preferable to wait until the heavy demand of the summer season was easing off somewhat. The summer timetable of those days normally ended about the middle of September.

The engine chosen to inaugurate the new arrangements was, not without some significance perhaps, No 1169 *Lord Faringdon*. The distinguished gentleman after whom this engine was named had been appointed Deputy Chairman of the LNER a short time before, and since the engine was to work into the heart of 'foreign' territory at Kings Cross the choice was almost certainly a deliberate piece of advertising on the part of those in charge at Immingham, in view of his long service as Chairman of the Great Central.

The popularity of the excursions meant heavy loads, and though no official details of coaching arrangements have been traced for this early period, study of photographs reveals trains of 14 or 15 vehicles, probably representing just about the heaviest loads worked by Great Central passenger engines in normal service. Hence the choice of *Lord Faringdon* was also desirable on grounds of power. Immingham had operated its summer season service with three of the type, but in September No 1164 was sent to Gorton for overhaul and later replaced by No 1167. This latter engine had spent about three months working on the Great Northern section from Kings Cross Loco, and had had a somewhat eventful stay there, having arrived as No 1167 *Lloyd George* and then losing its name during August for reasons which have never been fully explained, but which appear to have had more to do with party politics than railway matters. No exact date for the arrival of No 1167 at Immingham can be given, but it was noted working a Kings Cross turn as late as 8 September, and so must have been transferred after this date. Its arrival meant that the Immingham 'B3' strength was again up to three, easily sufficient to cover the newly-introduced working to London now that the summer season was over, though it should be remembered that the shed had other turns on which it liked to use 'B3s' when possible, the main one being the midday Leicester train mentioned in the *Grimsby News* extract earlier. Compared with such jobs the excursions ranked as less important, if only because they ran intermittently instead of daily.

The driver of *Lord Faringdon* on this auspicious inauguration was, if local legend is to be believed, Sid Cleaver, always remembered at Immingham as the first GCR driver to lodge at Kings Cross after

working through to London with an Eason special. As for the condition his engine was in, w can imagine that no effort was spared to put on a big a show as possible for the benefit of the Grea Northern onlookers at Kings Cross, now officiall part of the same railway but still regarded by th Great Central men as the opposition. No 1169 ha only recently returned from a general overhaul a Gorton, and as well as being in the pink o mechanical condition would have been give extra-special attention by the Imminghar cleaners, no doubt working under carefu instructions from above.

Notes for the remainder of 1923 ar unfortunately sparse, but the indications are tha 'B3' engines were being used regularly on th London turn. No 1168 *Lord Stuart of Wortley* wa noted on the Thursday following *Lord Faringdon* appearance, and the latter was back again on th second Thursday in October. A fortnight after tha however there appears to have been a hitch in th proceedings, with Atlantic No 1409 of Ne England Loco arriving at Kings Cross following failure of the rostered GCR engine; nothing known as to the identity of the crew, but it may b imagined that they were somewhat chagrined t find themselves arriving on a Great Norther engine in front of the spectators at Kings Cross

On 13 December a change of engine type recorded, one of many in the eventful history o the Cleethorpes-Kings Cross specials. The 'B 4-6-0s have received little attention in railwa writings, and it is therefore a great interest to not the appearance of No 196 on this Decembe Thursday. The 'B1s' were among the oldest o GCR two-cylinder designs, dating from 1903, an the use of this type on an Eason's special wa probably a move born of necessity, for at this tim two of Immingham's 'B3s' were under repair a Gorton, leaving none to spare for the Londo working. 'B1' No 196 had recently returned t Immingham after an overhaul at Gorton and s would have been in the best of condition, but i view of the marked difference in power betwee the 'B1' and 'B3' 4-6-0s, and the fact that No 19 was still running in its original form with saturate boiler and slide-valves, the running forema cannot have been very happy about the situatio especially as the load in this immedia pre-Christmas period is likely to have been a heav one. Unfortunately no details of arrival times we recorded.

The shortage of 'B3s' continued into the ne year and so there was nothing for it but to rost the 'B1' for further workings to London; both o the class were stationed at Immingham at th period, but it was some time since No 195 ha received an overhaul and it is likely to have bee very much a second choice; at all events, no not f it appearing in London have been traced. No 196 is noted twice more during January, and it remained on the scene right up to the middle of May although 'B3s' also took a share in the work, with No 1169 doing another spell between March and May. It was the latter which worked the Grimsby Cup Final excursion of Saturday 26 April. The last recorded appearance of No 196 was on Saturday 17 May, but by this time changes were taking place at Immingham Loco which were to have a considerable effect on the excursions. These will be described presently.

Early in 1924 a change had been made in the working of the excursions whereby instead of commencing at Grimsby Town as formerly they were advertised to start from Cleethorpes. In pre-Grouping days GNR trains had penetrated no further east than Grimsby because the line to Cleethorpes was Great Central property, and so the London excursions started and finished at Grimsby Town; passengers travelling from Cleethorpes had to catch a connecting train and change at the former. A trial had been made on 29 September when the excursion of that day, worked by No 1169 Lord Faringdon as described earlier, started from Cleethorpes, but subsequent trains reverted to Grimsby. However there was a good deal to recommend the idea of a Cleethorpes start, since as well as offering better facilities for those living in the vicinity it simplified the working as the coaches had in any case to be brought empty from Cleethorpes. A new arrangement therefore came into effect from Thursday 17 January whereby the Cleethorpes start was made permanent. A slight disadvantage was that the engine working was now somewhat more complicated, as after arriving at Cleethorpes chimney-first from Immingham Loco the engine had to work tender-first over the three miles to Grimsby Town, where it then reversed to gain the GNR line; the reader will find this easier to follow with the aid of the sketch-plan. The same manoeuvres took place on the return journey. Because of the tender-first working speeds on the rather tortuous Cleethorpes-Grimsby section were low, 11 or 12 minutes usually being allowed, although this included a call at Grimsby Docks station. With the London specials now regularly advertised as starting and finishing at Cleethorpes, they had acquired the form which they were to retain right through to their abandonment at the outbreak of World War 2.

One of the most interesting developments of early LNER days, as far as GCR locomotives are concerned, was the transfer of Class B3 engines to the Great Northern section, already mentioned briefly in connection with No 1167 and still in full

flow during 1924. Though the moves did not all take place at the same time, they had the eventual effect of bringing to an end the appearances of Class B3 engines on the London excursions, as by the end of April Immingham Loco had in effect surrendered its entire allocation, except for No 1168 which lingered until June; No 1167 was still officially allocated there until August, but was under repair from April. To persevere with the elderly 'B1s' was hardly a satisfactory solution in view of the expectation of increased loadings during the forthcoming summer season, and so more suitable replacements were urgently required. They arrived during May in the impressive shape of a trio of 'B7s', a type which could claim to be the most modern as well as the most powerful of Gorton-designed 4-6-0s. A more marked contrast with the 'B1s' could hardly be imagined, and though strictly classed as mixed-traffic engines they were in fact regularly used on passenger work, as their employment on the London specials indicates. In this sphere they were capable of excellent work, at times equalling that of the 'B3s', and were well liked by most Great Central men despite a reputation for heavy coal consumption; no doubt this was regarded by the Running Department as a small price to pay for the advantages of having such powerful and versatile engines available. For the London specials they were in many ways an ideal choice, capable of starting the heavy trains without difficulty, able to cope with the speeds required, and easily strong enough to surmount the only severe gradient which the route offered – that of Holloway Bank on the exit from Kings Cross.

The three engines which Immingham received were Nos 5469, 5482 and 5484, No 5469 previously based at Woodford and the other two from Gorton. This pair were of particular interest, being among the last of the class; the final batch of 'B7s', built from August 1923 onwards and sometimes referred to as 'Super B7s' were different from the earlier engines in having noticeably shorter chimneys and an altered profile to the outside cylinders. No 5484 was virtually brand-new when it arrived at Immingham, having been completed only in the previous March, and has historic interest in being the last of a long line of Gorton products.

A further point of interest about the two 'Super B7s' was that they had been put into traffic after the announcement of the new LNER numbering scheme, and carried their new numbers on large plates of the style formerly standard on all large GCR engines, combined with a painted version of the number of the tender in the approved LNER style. This unusual arrangement of cab and tender numbering, unique to a handful of Great Central engines, no doubt attracted plenty of attention at

Kings Cross, where the native GNR types were to be seen with plain cab sides, as laid down in the new LNER specification. Those in charge at Immingham Loco, not to mention the crews working to London, must have enjoyed the opportunity of participating in another piece of Great Central 'advertising', as well as showing off one of Gorton's latest products.

The first recorded appearance of one of the newly allocated 'B7s' was on Saturday 24 May, when No 5482 worked to Kings Cross. This was an occasion of some historic interest inasmuch as it was almost certainly the first time that a Class B7 engine had been seen at the GNR terminus. A week later came the turn of No 5484, bringing in a train of nine GCR coaches and two GNR diners. This was evidently a day of heavy demand as No 5469 was also noted at Kings Cross, having probably worked in with a second portion of the excursion. The holiday season was now getting well into its stride, and on Thursday 19 June another pair of 'B7s' was seen, this time Nos 5482 and 5484. A week later No. 5484 was back again, this time in the company of a 'stranger', No 5464 of Woodford; at this period Woodford engines were working regularly to Immingham on fish empties[2], and on a day of heavy traffic it sometimes happened that a visiting engine had to be borrowed to fill a gap on the roster board, particularly as there were so few 'B7s' on the permanent allocation. This is probably the explanation behind an appearance of No 5469 on a Cleethorpes special in full GCR livery and numbering; by the time it reached Immingham in 1924 it would almost certainly have been renumbered, having received an overhaul at Gorton beforehand, and its appearance at Kings Cross in earlier condition suggests that on that occasion it had been taken off a Woodford diagram whilst allocated there during 1923. No 5484 made regular appearances during July, being noted on three successive weeks, and No 5469 was also on the scene, on one occasion in the company of another stranger, Gorton's No 5078. Once again it was not uncommon to find Gorton 'B7s' making appearances on the Cleethorpes trains as there was a substantial pool of the class in Manchester and engines were often released for short periods to help other sheds at busy times.

Probably the most interesting event of August was another appearance of a 'B1', this time No 5195. It arrived at Kings Cross on Thursday the 21st of the month, assisted by a GNR 4-4-0, No 64, thought to have been allocated at the time to New England. The use of an assistant engine, presumably from Peterborough, suggests that the 'B1' was having problems with what is likely to have been a fairly sizeable load given the time of year, and once again points to the fact that the

two-cylinder 4-6-0s are hardly likely to have been the Immingham foreman's first choice for the London workings. No further notes of them have been traced apart from an undated reference in the Railway Magazine of May 1925 and it is probable that their brief heyday on the Cleethorpes specials if such it can be called, was over well before the spring of 1925. Both engines of the class received repairs at Gorton early in 1926 and were then transferred away from Immingham, never to return. So far as can be traced they never again appeared at Kings Cross in the period covered by this book, and so their short spell of work on the Cleethorpes excursions is of some historic interest for during their long career they do not appear to have strayed very often from their native GCR metals.

From the autumn of 1924 onwards notes are much more sparse, though entries in the contemporary Railway Magazine make it clear that the 'B7s' continued to monopolise the workings for some time, even though changes in the allocation brought some new faces to the scene. When No 5482 went to Gorton for repair in the autumn of 1925 it was never returned to Immingham, and the same thing happened to it sister engine, No 5484, early in 1926. In exchange Immingham received Nos 5477 in November 1925 and 5459 the following February. By the time No 5484 went to Gorton it had accumulated a total of 70,000 miles in service, almost all of it while working from Immingham Loco and including many trips on the Cleethorpes specials – its last recorded one was on Thursday 16 April 1925. In January 1926 the third of the original Immingham trio, No 5469, also went in for repair but was sent back again during April to soldier on alongside its new stablemates.

During this period the Immingham crews had ample opportunity to become thoroughly acquainted with the 'B7s', and it is a pity that no word-of-mouth account of their experiences on the Cleethorpes workings has survived. Though the firemen may on occasion have had to exert themselves somewhat, we can be sure that the ample reserve of power would be much appreciated, particularly when there was a substantial load behind the tender; footplate comfort was also a feature of these machines, with the steady riding that was so characteristic of Great Central engines being supplemented by the advantages of a side-window cab.

By the mid-1920s the Immingham men were of course well settled on the London duty and fully used to such rigours as it imposed. The main one of course was lodging – a long time was spent away from home, and there was a consequent degree of boredom during the stayover of more than 12 hours in London, though of course there was no hortage of diversions within easy reach of Kings Cross shed. From start to finish the whole round trip occupied a grand total of about 28 hours, this including preparation time before the morning departure from Immingham Loco, and probably some disposal time at the end of the duty; in the event therefore, most men may well have preferred to spend their hours at Kings Cross in bed. For those who lived at Grimsby, as quite a number of Immingham footplate staff did, further time was of course taken up in getting to and from the shed. The original idea was that Drivers Cleaver and Croft should alternate on the Thursday and Saturday workings, as has already been mentioned, but with the growing popularity of the excursions and consequent resort to the running of extra portions they were not infrequently called upon the work two trips in succession.

On arrival in London the Immingham engine ran light up to Kings Cross Loco and was then berthed there to await its return trip. This brought the hardest spell of work for the locomotive, as at the start the heavy train had to be humped up the 1 in 107 of Holloway Bank, which began at the platform end and continued through the Gasworks and Copenhagen Tunnels, both notorious for their treacherous rails. It was usual for the native GNR trains to have the use of an assistant engine when loads were heavy, and with the 13- and 14-coach assemblies it is probable that similar assistance was often provided for the Cleethorpes excursions. In addition to the job of getting up the bank, the crew also had quite a heavy responsibility in observing signals, for departure always took place in the hours of darkness and the Immingham men could not be expected to achieve the same familiarity as the native Great Northern men with the many complicated gantries out to Finsbury Park and beyond. It was often remarked that their approach to Kings Cross on up trains was always much more cautious than that of the Great Northern drivers, who seemed by comparison to sail down the bank with little regard for the fact that they might, as one Immingham man put it, 'finish up in the Thames'.

During its wait at Kings Cross the Immingham engine was not infrequently commandeered by the shed foreman to work extra trips at times of heavy traffic; during the summer season of 1927 Immingham 'B7s' were used on at least two occasions to work the 2.30pm Kings Cross-Hitching stopping train, which called at all stations north of Hatfield to reach Hitchin at 3.34. On Saturday 27 August 'B7' No 5459 was observed on this, and exactly a fortnight later 'B7' No 5072 appeared. The Kings Cross engine normally used on this working is believed to have returned from Hitchin on a train leaving at 5.55pm, and one

imagines that during the 2½ hour wait the Immingham visitor must have looked not a little out of place among the usual collection of Great Northern engines at Hitchin Loco. Though not actually observed on the up Cleethorpes trains, the 'B7s' would have worked into Kings Cross on LNER-organised excursions leaving Cleethorpes about 7am; during the height of the summer season the LNER appears to have acquired a temporary monopoly of the London excursions, with Eason's mainly restricted to the Thursday trains. By 1927 the pattern was for the LNER to advertise excursions to London every Saturday from about the middle of July to mid-September, and this prevailed for many years.

During such busy periods the excursions often ran in more than one part, which meant that special crewing arrangements had to be made. Apart from the two men mentioned earlier, the road knowledge of Immingham drivers did not extend south of Peterborough, and so they were either relieved at this point, or provision was made for a change of engine, the Immingham engine and men waiting at New England Loco for the return excursion. Because of the heavy demand it was also necessary for engines to be transferred temporarily to Immingham as the shed did not have enough of its own to cover all the extra trains. A further complication was that the demand could sometimes occur at other times of the year, as for instance on Saturday 20 October 1928, when no fewer than five special excursions were run between Grimsby and Kings Cross in connection with a League match played between Grimsby Town and Tottenham Hotspur at White Hart Lane; of these, three were full-day excursions, and in its report the *LNER Magazine* was at pains to point out that 'this was not an organised "Supporters" Club Outing or such event, the passengers being followers of the club and others induced to travel for various reasons, not one of the least being the attractiveness of the rail arrangements.'[5] Such a description indicates the extent to which the London excursions had become a part of daily life in Grimsby and district, and the original conception of J. W. Eason is clearly evident – nearly all seats were booked in advance and close on a thousand meals were served en route. Nothing is known of the engine or crewing arrangements on this occasion, but it is very clear that the event created a good deal of work for the Immingham shed foreman.

More than a year before the occasion just described had occurred, there was the first of further changes in the locomotive situation at Immingham. In the early months of 1927 the Class

B3 4-6-0s were sent back to the GC section following their spell on the GN, and this resulted in the return to Immingham of No 6168 *Lord Stuart of Wortley* in May, after an absence of a little less than three years. It remained the only representative of its class in Lincolnshire for over 12 months and was then transferred away again after one of its rather frequent repairs at Gorton Works. Nothing has survived to indicate whether or not it ever worked the London excursions during this second spell of residence, though as the solitary 'B3' it may well have been rostered regularly for the midday Leicester working already mentioned, which was something of a 'star turn' at Immingham. However, its stay in that part of the world, relatively short though it may have been, proved to be a sign of things to come, for in the middle of December 1928 two further 'B3s' moved in within the space of three days. The first of these was No 6164 *Earl Beatty*, the original Immingham-based 'B3' of GCR days, and then followed a distinguished newcomer, No 6165 *Valour*. The latter was a specially esteemed member of the class because of its status as the company's war memorial engine, and was always kept well cleaned and polished[4]. At this period it appears also to have been in original GCR condition apart from the standard LNER green livery and numbering.

To counterbalance these arrivals the 'B7' engines were moved away during the succeeding spring and summer, but in what seems to have been an immediate reversal of policy were replaced almost at once by other engines of the same class. The departure of the original 'B7s' meant that No 5469 finally severed its association with Immingham Loco after a stay of over five years, the only large six-coupled engine to have had a settled spell there up to this time. The number of 'B7s' was not quite made up to the original, as the three departed ones gave way to only two newcomers, Nos 5467 and 5478, but these were to have a lengthy spell at Immingham, and though playing very much a second fiddle to the 'B3s', were by no means eclipsed on the London excursions.

The new phase of 'B3' workings into London was no doubt well under way by the time of the earliest surviving note, Saturday 8 June 1929, when No 6165 *Valour* was photographed at the head of a typical 14 coach excursion. This engine and No 6164 are likely to have monopolised the workings for long periods of time during that year, though there are no notes to confirm this. During the busy weeks of July, August and early September of course we can be sure that the faithful 'B7s' were often called on to help out with the usual Saturday excursions, although the only note which has been traced is that of No 5478 on 14

September. In the following year, a series of observations extending through March and April shows the two 'B3s' working regularly to London, both on the usual mid-morning arrival and the afternoon half-day excursion, the latter having by this date become a familiar feature. After *Valour* had appeared on Thursday 6 March with Bill Croft at the regulator, the same engine was noted four more times between then and the end of April, while *Earl Beatty* made four recorded appearances during the same period, including a Cup Final excursion on Saturday 26 April, when it arrived at 10.30am with Driver Cleaver in charge.

During the middle of May a third 'B3' arrived at Immingham, sent fresh from overhaul at Gorton Works. This was No 6169 *Lord Faringdon*, notable as the engine originally chosen to pioneer the very first working from Cleethorpes to Kings Cross. Its transfer to Immingham was probably triggered by the fact that at this time No 6165 was out of traffic for repairs, but when the latter arrived back during June *Lord Faringdon* was allowed to remain, thus giving Immingham three 'B3s' for the first time since 1923. The first recorded trip of No 6169 to Kings Cross in this spell of service was on Saturday 14 June, when it brought in a half-day excursion at the usual time of 2.40pm, just over a month after being put back into traffic following its repair. *Valour* arrived back from Gorton Works a few weeks later, and the trio of 'B3s' were put to good use on what was evidently a very busy Thursday, 7 August, when they were all seen in Kings Cross, the spectacle they presented no doubt being all the more impressive for the fact that Nos 6165 and 6169 had so recently returned from overhaul; all three engines were resplendent in LNER green, and by this stage had their numbers on the cab side following the revised livery instructions issued late in 1928. The three are believed to have been carrying the controversial flowerpot chimney at this time, an LNER-designed fitting which has often been described in books as ugly, but which in the opinion of many contemporary observers did not detract in any way from their appearance. Unlike the other two, *Valour* apparently escaped the change of chimney for some time, and is thought not to have received this symbol of LNER ownership until its repair of 1930, long after the original Robinson chimneys had vanished from most GCR engines.

At about this time a decision had been put into effect whereby two further drivers, Fred East and Paul Leake, were taught the road through to Kings Cross. 'Eastie', as the former was inevitably known at Immingham, is remembered as a man blessed with rather less than perfect health, being a sufferer from stomach ulcers; when at work he was often to be seen leaning over the cab side, spitting and sometimes vomiting, but by all accounts this disposition did not in any way interfere with his [ab]ilities as an engineman, and he enjoyed a senior [p]osition at Immingham for many years. He is also [re]membered as the driver who, with Fireman [H]arold Hutton, had the embarrassment of running [o]ut of coal while working an Eason's train in the [vi]cinity of Hornsey Loco, some miles short of [K]ings Cross; no doubt a few caustic remarks were [p]assed at Hornsey about the coal-consuming [p]ropensities of his engine, a 'B7' 4-6-0, after [a]ssistance had been summoned from the nearby [sh]ed.

Paul Leake's career included an accident at [C]leethorpes on Friday 31 July 1925 whilst he was [a]cting as pilotman to a Driver W. Harley on a [fo]rmer Great Eastern engine, 'J20' No 8281. The [a]ccident occurred during shunting operations as [th]e engine was marshalling coaches to work as [e]mpty stock from Cleethorpes to Kings Cross, and [re]sulted in injury to Driver Harley. Whether [D]river Leake was to blame is not known, but his [se]lection as a regular driver for the London [ex]cursions indicates that he was not penalised in [a]ny way.

The decision to train these extra drivers may [h]ave sprung from the growing popularity of the [L]ondon excursions, but could have been simply a [lo]ng-term measure in anticipation of the eventual [re]tirement of Drivers Cleaver and Croft; in any [e]vent the fact that there were now four drivers [fa]miliar with the road through to Kings Cross [in]stead of the original two would have been a great [a]dvantage at busy times. As to when the new men [fir]st worked through to London, no precise dates [a]re available, but Fred East is known to have [b]rought a train into Kings Cross on Thursday 27 [M]arch 1930, when he arrived at 10.30am with No [6]165 *Valour*.

The reader will by now be getting used to the [fa]ct that for some mysterious reason the 'B3' [e]ngines were never allowed to remain for very long [a]t Immingham, and in the period from late 1930 up [t]o the spring of 1933 there were several moves [b]ackwards and forwards, with engines usually [d]eparting at the close of the summer season, [so]metimes due for repair, and returning in the [fo]llowing spring or summer; probably the seasonal [n]ature of the Eason's and other excursion [w]orkings accounts for this. The one curious [ex]ception was No 6169 *Lord Faringdon*, which for [so]me reason remained a fixture throughout this [p]eriod, and it even seems to have escaped the [fr]equent visits to Gorton Works which were rather [a] feature of the 'B3' class history. The various [m]oves to and from Immingham involved only four [o]f the class, as by this time the other two, Nos 6166 [E]arl Haig and 6168 *Lord Stuart of Wortley* had [b]een rebuilt with Caprotti valves, which meant [th]ey could not be sent to Immingham because the specially trained fitters needed to maintain the patent valve gear were available only at Gorton and Neasden.

The period 1930-33 is not well covered as far as observations are concerned, and with the onset of harder times consequent on the slump it is possible that the excursions did not operate with the same frequency as in previous years. In the spring of 1931 No 6169 *Lord Faringdon* was seen at Kings Cross twice, on Saturday 25 April with a train of 13 coaches, and then a fortnight later on an afternoon arrival with 12 coaches. The former was Cup Final day, always a popular occasion for excursions regardless of which teams were taking part, and a similar Cup Final excursion was noted in the following year, on 24 April when No 6167 arrived at Kings Cross with 14 coaches.

During this same period the London excursions gained a most unexpected share of the limelight when a run on one of the trains was published by the late Cecil J. Allen in his monthly *Railway Magazine* feature, 'British Locomotive Practice & Performance.' In an article devoted mainly to the running of the LNER Pacifics, he has this to say:

'The fourth column introduces a most interesting comparison, in the working of one of the large four-cylinder Great Central 4-6-0 engines – No. 6169 *Lord Faringdon* – to London on a heavy express excursion from Grimsby. This is about the best performance that I have ever seen recorded with one of these locomotives, and compares very favourably with the adjacent Pacific efforts. Driver W. Croft, of Immingham, was in charge. Intermediate speeds were 65 m.p.h. at Holme, 49 at Ripton, 70½ at Huntingdon and Offord, 62½ – a splendid figure – at St Neot's, 68½ at Tempsford, 56 at Langford, 61 at Three Counties, 50 at Hitchin and 43 at Stevenage. All this was quite of the best Pacific quality until the slight falling-off at the top of the rise to Stevenage. Unfortunately the whole of the run inwards from Welwyn was badly checked by signals; otherwise there is no reason to doubt that No. 6169 would have reached London with this 460-ton train in 80 minutes from Peterborough – a feat on which Driver Croft may well congratulate himself.'

The 'B3' engines were not a class about which, as a general rule, Mr Allen had a great deal to say in his 'Practice & Performance' articles, and the same can also be said of crews from Immingham Loco; the above extract is therefore of a certain rarity, and is reproduced here for that reason. Its most salient message would appear to be that a 'B3' in good hands was capable of work not far short of that done by the LNER Pacifics.

From Mr Allen's remarks it can also be seen that on the section south of Peterborough the London excursions were timed to the best LNER express standards, this being necessary in order to prevent them obstructing other trains. A schedule of 1935 shows that in the up direction they were allowed 1 hour 28 minutes for the 87 miles from Peterborough to Kings Cross, and 1 hour 35 minutes coming back, both comparing closely with the GNR main line trains. On the Cleethorpes–Peterborough section the times were much restricted by the stops which were made, usually at Louth, Boston and Spalding, and the tender-first working between Cleethorpes and Grimsby was also an inhibiting factor, besides including a stop at Grimsby Docks. The passenger thus sampled some interesting contrasts; having been first taken at a snail's pace along the tortuous section to Grimsby, with the train snaking gingerly round the severe left-hand curve beyond Riby Street Platform and then swinging equally sharply to the right over Garden Street crossing, he later found himself being whirled along the Great Northern main line at Pacific speeds. Frequent level crossings were a feature of the short run into Grimbsy, among them the one over Cleethorpe Road, reputedly the busiest in England with 'nearly 40 trains passing every hour of the day'.

It appears that the fast Peterborough-Kings Cross schedule did not always enable the excursions to keep completely clear of Great Northern section trains as there is a report in the *Railway Magazine,* submitted by no less a contributor than the Earl of Sandwich, to the effect that the 9.30am Huntingdon-Kings Cross train, normally a Grantham Pacific working at the time when the Earl was writing, was delayed by signal checks on 17 journeys out of a total of 25, most of these occurring on Thursdays when the Huntingdon train was preceded by an Eason's special. The delay may of course have been caused by the special being impeded by other trains ahead of it, rather than losing time on its own account, for it is clear that it was slotted into a very busy morning timetable.

On the Cleethorpes-Peterborough stretch the overall time was 1 hour 40 minutes for the 80 miles, giving an average speed somewhat below that booked south of Peterborough. The stops were of very short duration, usually one or two minutes except for that at Grimsby Town, where as described earlier the engine had to change ends; five minutes were allowed for this manoeuvre, and during that time the gates at Wellowgate crossing, on the other side of the station, remained closed because it was occupied by the standing train.

By the early 1930s the Cleethorpes specials, in common with other LNER trains of the same type, were beginning to display certain small differences. Reporting numbers were now being carried by the engines, so that signalmen and other staff could identify special trains more easily. In previous practice working numbers had been allotted in the special notices but these had never been displayed on the actual trains, and the reform was evidently aimed at eliminating confusion. Usually mounted on the top lamp-iron ahead of the chimney, the numbers were made up of individual digits carried on small boards and displayed in groups of two or three as the train numer required, securely retained in a special bracket. A somewhat similar system came into use at about the same time on the GWR, where the engines of all fast trains were to be seen carrying very large numbers on the smokebox door, but an important difference was that whereas the LNER numbers were simply issued at random on the weekly notices, their GWR equivalents were in the form of a code, each digit conveying information about the route, time of the train, and number of portions. The LNER system appears to have operated on a somewhat haphazard basis, special trains often running without their distinguishing number, presumably because of a shortage of number boards at the station of origin, or perhaps simply because such details were sometime overlooked in the rush to mount an additional portion of a special at the last minute; sometime the number was chalked on the engine smokebox. Occasionally the special numbers were followed by letters, but the significance of these addenda is not known.

Carriage stock was also changing. Early photos of the Cleethorpes specials show a motley collection of vehicles, with a mixture of former GCR and GNR coaches marshalled round a large GNR diner, probably a survival from the days of Great Northern operation. As new stock was gradually introduced on to LNER expresses, other vehicles were downgraded on to secondary duties and by the mid-1930s Gresley-type stock was in evidence on the Cleethorpes trains, giving them a much more uniform appearance. Several witnesses have remarked that on the Eason's trains special roofboards were carried, and this is also mentioned in the contemporary *Railway Magazine,* but no information is available as to how regular this practice was, or when it began, nor is it possible to say what the wording was. One author has claimed that the Eason's specials carried headboards, but no confirmation of this has ever been found.

Make-up of the coaching stock as given in the 1935 notices was: brake third, five corridor thirds, two open thirds, restaurant car, pantry car, and another brake third, the coaches being marshalled in that order; the absence of first-class ccommodation will be noted, a most unusual feature for main-line trains, though not of course for specials. The total of 11 coaches would of course be increased at busy times by the addition of strengthening vehicles.

Guards employed on the specials normally originated from Cleethorpes and are believed to have been diagrammed in the same way as the enginemen, booking on at their home station and travelling through to Kings Cross to lodge. It is not known how many Cleethorpes guards knew the road through to London, but it is believed that on occasions when several trains were running the extra workings were arranged in a similar way to the enginemen's, with Cleethorpes guards working through to Peterborough and being relieved there by GNR section men. Unfortunately none of the names of the Cleethorpes guards has been traced.

During 1933 came yet another round of changes on the locomotive scene, bringing into the picture two classes which had not previously been concerned with the Cleethorpes excursions. The Class B4 engines had nearly all been based on the GN section from about 1925, but as more LNER types began to appear on the scene during the early 1930s some of them found their way back into the former Great Central lines. No 6095 had been at Immingham since just before the end of 1932, and in the middle of the following March it was followed by Nos 6101 and 6103, these arrivals replacing the two 'B3s' currently stationed at Immingham, No 6165 and the trusty No 6169 Lord Faringdon. Unfortunately no records of 'B4s' on the London excursions have been traced, but it is virtually certain that they were used on them since the engines which replaced them a few months later undoubtedly did this work. As to why the 'B4s' should have had such a short stay in Lincolnshire, nothing is known; superheated in the years following Grouping, they had done excellent work during their time at Copley Hill and Ardsley Locos, mainly on the difficult road between Leeds and Doncaster – many of them were still employed in this role at the outbreak of war. Yet they had left Immingham within a matter of months, and there is evidence that even during that short time they were not the first choice for the excursion workings, as on Saturday 20 May 'B7' No 5467 was noted on a half-day excursion, and 'B7' No 5478 similarly on Saturday 17 June. No 'B4s' were ever stationed at Immingham again apart from a very short spell in 1937 when No 6095 and another engine had a few weeks there.

Their replacements were Class B2 engines, visually one of the most distinctive types ever to emerge from Gorton. The 'Cities' had often visited Immingham in the course of their various workings but had never previously been allocated there and the first arrival, No 5426 City of Chester, had never been stationed anywhere apart from Gorton and Sheffield up to that time. It arrived in early May, and was followed in June by two more of the class, No 5425 City of Manchester and No 5423 Sir Sam Fay, and then in July by No 5428 City of Liverpool. It is curious that both these engines and the 'B4s' were of a considerably lower power class than the 'B3s' which had been so abruptly replaced earlier in the year, being of course two-cylinder engines as compared with the four cylinders of the 'B3s'. The only explanation which can be offered for this is that the trainloads may have become somewhat lighter during the early 1930s as a result of the depression, when most railway traffics fell off sharply. Nevertheless the 'B2s' are believed to have worked London excursions of at least 11 vehicles, and so far as is known never failed to give every satisfaction on this work. It should however be noted that, following an overhaul at Gorton, the ever-faithful Lord Faringdon came back to Immingham in late June for a three-month spell, evidently to lend a hand with the high-season workings. It is probably that it found its chief employment on the Leicester turn referred to earlier in this chapter.

The earliest sighting traced of a 'B2' on the London excursions is Saturday 21 October, when No 5428 City of Liverpool was seen at Kings Cross. Such visitations were not of course the first time engines of the class had been seen in the Great Northern terminus, as at least one of them had worked through from Gorton in the days of the short-lived Sheffield Pullman soon after Grouping, and they had also been used by Sheffield for excursions into Kings Cross.

Unfortunately, notes of their working from Immingham are very scarce, and after the date given above there is no further record until Saturday 14 April 1934, when two of the class were seen at Kings Cross, No 5423 Sir Sam Fay and No 5428 City of Liverpool. Cup Final day two weeks later saw 'B7' No 5478 arriving from Cleethorpes, probably with a load too heavy for a 'B2', but the latter were back in the act once more by 12 May, when City of Liverpool again worked into Kings Cross on an afternoon LNER excursion.

In a further series of moves which are just as difficult to explain as those which brought the 'B2s' to Immingham, the much-travelled 'B3' engines came back for a third spell of service in the spring of 1935. No 6164 Earl Beatty was noted leaving Kings Cross in the very early morning of Sunday 16 June with Sid Cleaver on the footplate, beginning its return journey to Cleethorpes. This engine had arrived at Immingham on 13 April, accompanied by the unnamed No 6167 which had completed a general repair at Gorton at the end of March. These moves naturally saw the departure of most of the 'B2' engines, Nos 5425, 5426 and 5428 having in fact already left by the end of February, but for some reason *Sir Sam Fay* remained behind, and was still to be found at Immingham when the war started – a remarkably consistent record at a shed which, as the reader will by now be aware, seemed fated to have its passenger engines moved about rather frequently. It is perhaps something of a coincidence that Immingham had close associations with the great Sir Sam Fay, as he had received his knighthood from King George V at the opening of the nearby docks in 1912.

In December the passenger engine stud was further augmented by the return of the old favourite *Lord Faringdon,* and for the first time in a good many years the number of engines suitable for use on the London excursions rose once again to four. Early in the following January the number of 'B7s' was also increased, but as we have explained elsewhere[5] the members of this class were now mainly occupied on the new fish train diagram which Immingham Loco had acquired at about that time.

The 'B3s' remained in charge almost through to the outbreak of war, enjoying their longest continuous stint at Immingham. Notes of their appearances on the London excursions have not been easy to come by, although they are known to have worked into Kings Cross with some regularity during this period, sometimes assisted by the solitary 'B2', *Sir Sam Fay*. Three sightings in the first fortnight of 1937 show No 6167 at work, bringing typical Thursday loads of 300 tons into Kings Cross on 7 and 14 January, and on the Saturday in between a train of 420 tons which included a portion from Gainsborough as well as the usual Cleethorpes coaches. Driver Paul Leake was in charge during the first of these two weeks, and then came the turn of a recent recruit to the elite band of London excursion drivers, George Emmerson, thought to have stepped up not very long before this because of the approaching retirement of one of the senior hands. Driver Emmerson was highly thought of at Immingham, and later on was promoted to the rank of Locomotive Inspector.

A note for Saturday 8 May shows *Sir Sam Fay* arriving in London on an afternoon excursion with a load of no fewer than 14 coaches. Due at 2.54pm, the engine reached Kings Cross only two minutes late with this huge train – a good example of the capabilities of the 'B2s' when in good hands.

By this period the main-line passenger engines at Immingham Loco were the recipients of just a little more extra-special care than in previous times. The long-drawn-out programme of LNER shed improvements had finally reached Imming-

ham in 1936, or about that time, was the buildir of a 'cenotaph' type coaling plant; once suc installations had been brought into use it was usu for the original hand coaling-stage to be retaine for emergencies only, but at Immingham th feature remained in full operation, now supplyir 'best' coal for passenger and fast goods engine only. As to why such preferential treatment shoul have been meted out, it can only be suggested tha at least in the case of the London excursio engines, the reason may have been a desire to pac the tenders as tightly as possible in order to have good reserve for the long run to Kings Cross. I principle it seems highly unlikely that there coul ever have been any difficulty about coal suppl with a tender capacity of seven tons on a run o barely 150 miles, but the incident described earlie involving Driver Fred East will be recalled. Th experience of having an engine run out of coal o the way to London was clearly a mo embarrassing one for all concerned, and had led t some angry exchanges at Immingham Loco. As result, extra care was always taken to ensure tha the engines should arrive at Kings Cross with a fa residue of coal in the tender, and at most shed hand coaling with usually considered the best wa of filling the tender to capacity, although t modern ears the idea of persisting with such a slo and labour-intensive method of doing the jo when a mechanical appliance was provided sound very strange.

'Best' coal at Immingham was normally Dalto Main, occasionally Maltby, and as at all sheds wa rigidly restricted to engines working on fa main-line duties. However, the Immingham crew were under no illusions about the fact that th 'best' coal was considerably inferior to that used a other sheds, particularly on the GCR main lin such as Leicester, where fast train engines wer fuelled with the outstanding Rother Vale coal 'six tubfuls would bring you all the way home fror Leicester', according to one Immingham man.

A further step in the direction of modernisatio though of a different kind, was taken in the sprin of 1938 when 'B3' No 6167 was sent to Gorton fc conversion to Caprotti valve-gear, following whic it returned most unusually to Immingham t become the only Caprotti-fitted engine ever t work there in prewar days. It has already bee mentioned that the practice was for the converte engines to be based either at Gorton or Neasde where trained fitters were available to service th gear, and the return of No 6167 to Immingham wa therefore something of an anomaly; perhaps it wa hoped that the gear fitted to this engine, which wa of an improved type, would not require th exceptionally frequent maintenance which th earlier design had needed, but the fact that N 6167 was transferred to Neasden in the followir ovember suggests that the idea was not a success. uring its short stay at Immingham, however, it d manage to put in at least one appearance on e London excursions, an event unusual enough merit a mention in the *Railway Observer*, ough unfortunately the date was not recorded. his was probably the only occasion up to that me that observers on the GNR main line had had e opportunity of seeing a Caprotti-fitted 'B3', as ey were otherwise confined entirely to the GCR.

Though it falls somewhat outside the scope of is chapter, it should be mentioned that in ddition to their Grimsby premises the firm of ason's also had a branch office in Lincoln, tuated on Cornhill, and from here railway xcursions to London and elsewhere were romoted in the same way as in Grimsby, except at the firm never seemed to advertise itself to uite the same extent, and appeared content to act mply as an agent for the LNER. Lincoln-London xcursions ran via two different routes, either rough Grantham and the Great Northern line or y way of Sleaford and Spalding to reach the main ne at Peterborough. Early in 1939 a scheme was operation whereby excursions from Lincoln ere worked to Spalding and then attached to the ear of half-day Eason's excursions from leethorpes, the ensemble being worked by a oncaster engine which had worked from Lincoln. Vhen this began, or how often it took place, is ow known for certain. On Saturday 4 February o 6169 *Lord Faringdon* came off the up leethorpes train at Spalding to give way to no less n engine than No 2744 *Grand Parade* from oncaster, the latter proceeding to London with a ombined train consisting of Cleethorpes and .incoln portions. *Lord Faringdon* is reported as aving remained at Spalding for the rest of the lay, presumably awaiting the return excursion. imilar events took place a fortnight later, when a oncaster 'Green Arrow', No 4788, worked to palding with the Lincoln excursion, replaced No 423 *Sir Sam Fay* on the Cleethorpes portion and vent through to Kings Cross with the combined rain, No 5423 remaining at Spalding as before. he advantage of such arrangements, obviously, vas that one engine could be diagrammed to do he work of two, and in the economic climate of 939 such developments were very desirable, but

in practice it is doubtful if such workings took place very often. The departure from Lincoln was much too late for the full-day excursion from Cleethorpes, and so at the best could only be combined with a Cleethorpes train when the latter ran on a half-day basis, which was not a regular arrangement.

Very few notes are available from 1939 apart from those just quoted, but the 'B3s' appear to have been in regular charge of the normal full-day workings from Cleethorpes. The best-recorded occasion is Cup Final day, 29 April, when Nos 6165 *Valour* and 6169 *Lord Faringdon* arrived at Kings Cross in the region of 10.30am with specials Nos 467 and 468 respectively; as well as the usual Cleethorpes coaches, Special No 467 contained a portion from Barton-on-Humber, and No 468 likewise from Brigg. Return in both cases was in the early hours of the morning.

The final development to be recorded in this story has a familiar ring about it, for it was nothing less than the transfer of the Immingham 'B3s' to a different shed and their replacement by 'B2s', exactly as in 1933. As before, no satisfactory reason can be offered for these frequent and apparently random exchanges. The new arrivals were the same three which had left in 1935, Nos 5425, 5426 and 5428; they came on the scene in mid-July, the very height of the summer season, and were no doubt soon put to regular use, but with the outbreak of war only a matter of weeks away it is perhaps not surprising that no notes of their work have come to light. The commencement of hostilities at the beginning of September put an abrupt end to the kind of joyriding typified by the Cleethorpes-London excursions, and when the trains were eventually restarted years later the engines which have dominated the story told in this chapter were in the shadow of the scrapheap.

Notes
1. George Dow, *Great Central, Vol III*, Chapter 3.
2. Jackson & Russell, *The Great Central in LNER Days*, Chapter 12.
3. *LNER Magazine*, December 1928.
4. See Chapter VII.
5. Jackson & Russell, *The Great Central in LNER Days*, Chapter 12.

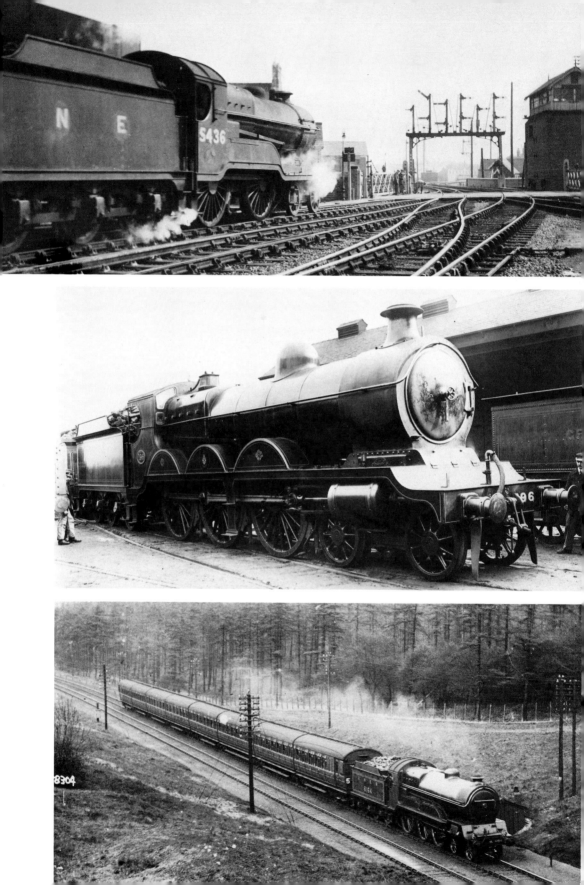

Left:
Garden Street level crossing, looking east from Grimsby Town station. The former GNR route to London can be seen curving away to the right beyond the signal gantry. 'D10' No 5436 *Sir Berkeley Sheffield* is signalled for the Cleethorpes line in this 1946 view. *Photo C. R. L. Coles*

Centre left:
In early LNER days the two Class B1 4-6-0s were tried on the Cleethorpes excursions. No 196 is pictured at Neepsend Loco, Sheffield, in pre-Grouping days. *Real Photos*

Bottom left:
A 'B3' on the East Coast main line. No 6164 *Earl Beatty* is seen on an up GN section working in the mid-1920s. *Photo H. Gordon Tidey*

Right:
Pride in the job. A trio of Immingham cleaners pose at the side of No 6168 *Lord Stuart of Wortley* after getting it ready for the midday working to Leicester. Passed Cleaner Bill Botham is seen at left. *I. Botham collection*

Below:
Almost new, one of the 1923 batch of 'B7s' on Gorton Loco, carrying its interim number 477C. *Real Photos*

Top:
'B7' No 5484 approaches Finsbury Park in April 1925 with an excursion from Cleethorpes. The GCR-style plate carrying the LNER number on the cab is apparent.
Photo F. R. Hebron/Rail Archive Stephenson

Above:
Passing Greenwood on the GNR main line on a summer's morning in 1924, 'B7' No 5469, still in GCR colours, heads an up Cleethorpes excursion.
Photo F. R. Hebron/Rail Archive Stephenson

Above right:
The 'Cities' began to appear on the Cleethorpes excursions in the early 1930s. No 5423 *Sir Sam Fay* has just passed Hawkshead bridge with an up train.
Photomatic

Right:
'B4' No 6101 had a short spell at Immingham in 1933 and may have been used on the Cleethorpes excursions. Here it is seen entering Kings Cross on 14 May 1938 with an excursion from the West Riding. *Photo L. Hanson*

Below:

A view of the busy level crossing at Cleethorpe Road, Grimsby, as seen on a Senior Service cigarette card. The picture is taken about 1936 and shows 'C4' No 5264 on an excursion from Cleethorpes. *H. Bowdur collection*

Right:

Reverse of Senior Service cigarette card.
H. Bowdur collection

POINT DUTY

BRITISH RAILWAYS

A SERIES OF 48 — No. 25

POINT DUTY

There can be very few traffic crossings in England where the policeman on point duty finds railway trains included in his regular traffic. This photograph shows the level crossing at Grimsby Docks station, which crosses the Grimsby–Cleethorpes road. This is said to be the busiest level crossing in England, and nearly 40 trains pass every hour during the day. Owing to the great dislocation of traffic the question of providing a bridge is now being discussed.

SENIOR SERVICE
CIGARETTES

Above:
'B2' No 5428 *City of Liverpool* **backs out of Kings Cross**
Platform 8 after arriving with an excursion.
Photo C. R. L. Coles

Below:
A typical Cleethorpes excursion of the late 1930s. 'B3' No
6167 is seen heading for London near Potter's Bar.
H. Bowdur collection

Above:
With special number clearly visible, No 6169 *Lord Faringdon* nears London on a Saturday excursion from Cleethorpes.   *Photo C. R. L. Coles*

Below:
In the background of this Immingham Loco group can be seen the reinforced concrete coaling stage, restricted to 'best' coal after the hopper had been built. In this view 'B5' No 5184 has evidently just been cleaned.
I. Botham collection

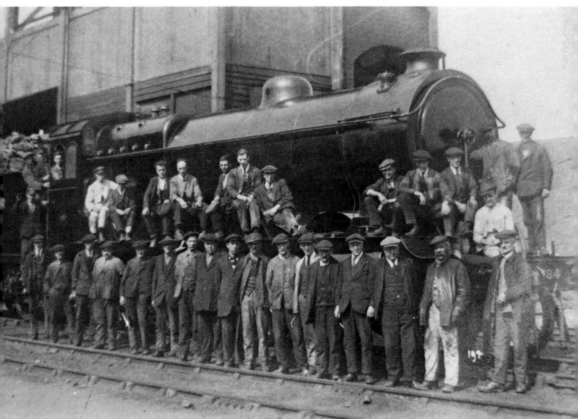

V
Milk for Marylebone

*'By about 1930 the old traffic in milk
churns on country branch lines had
practically ceased. No longer did the
farmer drive to the station and unload the
churns; instead, the churns were picked up
by lorries from a stand at the farm turning,
and taken to a creamery, and the milk sent
in glass-lined tanks to London, by train or
by road.'*

Charles Loch Mowat,
Britain Between the Wars

In the *Railway Magazine* of October 1933
appears a photograph showing a train of
some 16 or 17 tank wagons, property of
United Dairies Ltd, at Addison Road,
Kensington; at the head is a quite distinguished
member of the Great Western locomotive fleet,
'Saint' Class No 2973 *Robins Bolitho*. The
ensemble presents an impressive spectacle, and
one which by 1933 was becoming increasingly
common on our railways, as the above quotation
suggests. Within a short time of the picture being
taken, as this chapter tells, the GCR line was to
see the introduction of trains of this type. But first
we look at the origins of the bulk conveyance of
milk to London, and at some of the factors which
resulted in the appearance of the distinctive tank
wagons from the late 1920s onwards.

Milk had of course been transported by rail to
the capital for a great many years, by means of
churns loaded either into vehicles specially
provided for the purpose, or else in guards' vans –
the churns were a common sight on station
platforms all over the country. During the 1920s
however a degree of rationalisation began to
overtake the milk industry in London, which
became increasingly dominated by large-scale
concerns preparing milk in considerable quantities
both for domestic and other uses. They began to
supplant the small farm-based dairies which had
originally made domestic deliveries from a horse
and trap, the milk being deposited on the
customer's doorstep in a jug left out for the
purpose. There were various reasons for the
change – the small-scale dairymen were not always
able to compete effectively, farms in the vicinity of
London were gradually disappearing as new
housing and industrial estates sprang up on the
outskirts of the expanding city, and there was a
growing preference, on hygienic grounds, for the

bottled, pasteurised product supplied by the big
dairies over the farm milk delivered in an open
container. There was also the factor of greater
consumption to be taken into account; publicity
was increasingly given at this period to the
nutritional value of milk, and breakfast cereals
were becoming more popular. Even such things as
the growing popularity of milk chocolate helped to
promote milk consumption – Messrs Cadbury's,
the well-known chocolate manufacturers, used 12
million gallons of milk in 1931 as compared with
five million gallons in 1920[1]. In Government
circles the first moves were being made towards
the subsidising of school milk.

United Dairies typified the trend by
concentrating production in a large central depot
at Finsbury Park, on the LNER Great Northern
section not far from Kings Cross. By making full
use of the main-line rail facilities offered at this
location they were quickly able to expand
production, taking in supplies of milk from further
and further afield. To facilitate these operations
bulk tanks were soon brought into use.

The use of glass-lined tanks for storage and
conveyance of milk and other edible fluids is
believed to have originated in the USA. As early
as 1907 storage tanks of this type had been
imported from Rochester, New York, for
installation at the breweries of S. Allsopp & Sons,
Burton-on-Trent, and by that date the use of
similar tanks for bulk conveyance had already
begun, or was soon to do so [2]. So far as the milk
industry was concerned, the use of bulk tanks
conferred many advantages, particularly in the
elimination of the cumbersome handling processes
so necessary in dealing with churns; this not only
cut down labour costs, but also increased the speed
of transit, a very important consideration. Two
hygienic advantages were that the tanks were
insulated to keep the milk cool during journeys,
and the contents could be pumped in and out
without exposure to air.

History was made in both the railway and milk
industries when the first glass-lined tanks were put
into service in December 1927; considerable
publicity was given to the inaugural journeys of
these novel milk trains, working to London from
Wooton Bassett in Wiltshire and Calveley,
Cheshire. In its issue of January 1930 the *LNER
Magazine* announced that similar vehicles had
gone into service at United Dairies' Finsbury Park
depot in December 1928.

The original design of tank ran on four wheels,

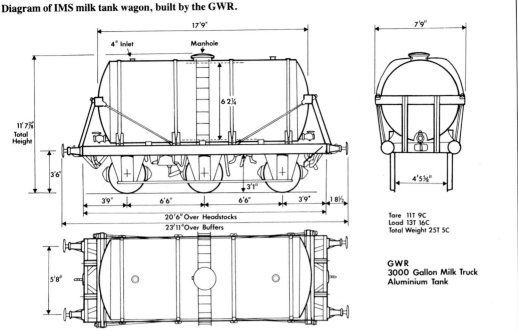

Diagram of IMS milk tank wagon, built by the GWR.

17'9"

4" Inlet   Manhole

6 2¼

11' 7⅞"
Total
Height

3'6"

3'1"

3'9"   6'6"   6'6"   3'9"   1 8½"

20'6" Over Headstocks
23'11" Over Buffers

5'8"

7'9"

4'5⅜"

Tare   11T 9C
Load 13T 16C
Total Weight 25T 5C

**GWR
3000 Gallon Milk Truck
Aluminium Tank**

but not long afterwards there was a move towards the use of a six-wheel chassis, probably on grounds of stability, and from 1933 all the original vehicles were remounted on six-wheel underframes as they went through the works for repairs. The firm which is the subject of this chapter acquired its first tank wagons in 1934, by which time there were regulations in force stipulating that all new vehicles must incorporate a six-wheel chassis.

By comparison with organisations such as United Dairies, the company was not much more than a small minnow in the national milk pond. Known as Independent Milk Supplies (IMS), it had been founded only in 1928 in what a milk industry magazine described as 'humble circumstances' – hardly a propitious beginning by the sound of it. Yet its development was so rapid that within only six years the company was planning to leave the modest establishment in Holloway and move to brand-new purpose-built premises in the fashionable western purlieus of London; this new factory was at no other address than Rossmore Road, Marylebone, immediately adjacent to the GCR terminus and directly accessible by rail. Its location between the passenger terminus and the carriage shed indicates clearly that the move had been made with the full knowledge and co-operation of the LNER, which was evidently anticipating new business to accrue from the arrangement. As a further benefit to the milk company, the new premises were located within a short distance of the West End, where it

had cultivated its most profitable markets.

Work on the construction of the dairy went ahead quickly, and by about 1935 the contractor, John Laing & Co, had completed what was at that time considered to be the most up-to-date dairy in London, initially capable of dealing with 1,600 gallons of milk per hour, and soon processing four times that amount. These statistics alone give a good indication of the phenomenal growth of IMS.

Circumstances undoubtedly conspired in the company's favour. The activities of the Milk Marketing Board, created in 1933 to assist the milk producers, brought about a stabilising of prices which greatly facilitated the operations of firms such as IMS. Other factors were the introduction of free school milk in 1934, and the commencement of a Government scheme to supply subsidised milk to nursing mothers and young children in depressed areas; a more indirect development, but of equal importance, was the return to a measure of prosperity from 1934 onwards, as well as the growth in demand that resulted simply from the ever-increasing population of London.

Most of the milk processed at the Rossmore Road plant came from two country dairies which IMS had purchased at about the time of moving to its new premises, one in Scotland and the other in Shropshire. Both these places were of course well

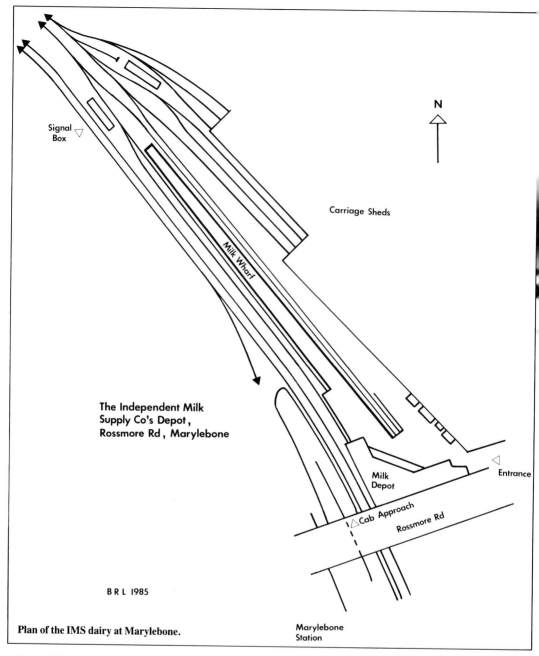

Signal
Box

N

Carriage Sheds

Milk Wharf

The Independent Milk
Supply Co's Depot,
Rossmore Rd, Marylebone

Milk
Depot

Entrance

Cab Approach

Rossmore Rd

BRL 1985

Plan of the IMS dairy at Marylebone.

Marylebone
Station

off the GC system, but the two traffics differed widely in the distance which they covered over Great Central metals on their way to Marylebone, and in this respect it was the Shropshire milk which was considerably the more important, and which forms the main theme of this chapter.

Dorrington is an attractive village on the A49 main road about seven miles due south of Shrewsbury, and it was here that a dairy was established in 1921 under the ownership of a concern known as Midland Farmers Ltd, in which most of the leading Shropshire dairy farmers had a share. The dairy's function was to receive milk in churns from the surrounding farms, cool it in special containers and make deliveries over a wide area; it was no doubt with a view to extending its scope as much as possible that the dairy was built directly alongside the goods yard at Dorrington station, on the Hereford-Shrewsbury Joint Line of the GWR and LMS: churns were sent by rail to hrewsbury and from there on to Paddington via he GWR main line through Birmingham. Midland armers Ltd got into financial difficulties in the early 1930s and went into liquidation; the business was eventually offered to the Milk Marketing Board in lieu of debts incurred, and arrangements were made for Independent Milk Supplies to take over the premises at Dorrington. The company duly assumed command in November 1935.

Under its new owners the dairy underwent certain structural alterations which included the building of offices on the upper floor, and its output was now redirected to Marylebone. At first the milk was still in churns, but plans were already afoot to modernise the traffic, and so it was that this charmingly rural spot was soon to be invaded by the shining new bulk tanks, symbol of the revolutionised milk industry.

It was however the Scottish dairy, situated at Sanquhar in Dumfries-shire, which saw the first use of the new-style IMS tank wagons. This traffic was already in full flow by the summer of 1935, and followed a most interesting route involving Glasgow & South Western metals from Sanquhar to Carlisle and then along the West Coast main line as far as Bletchley, where it was turned on to the LMS Bletchley-Oxford line to reach the GCR system at Verney Junction. The tank wagons normally ran in batches of three, and on their long journey over LMS metals were probably marshalled as part of a larger train – on the journey from Bletchley to Verney Junction for instance, they were attached to the rear of a local passenger train bound for Banbury. On the Great Central section they were conveyed in a similar manner, working first to Aylesbury on a stopping passenger train and then forward to Marylebone on one of the usual Aylesbury-Marylebone locals. Empty tanks followed the same route in reverse, being worked to Verney Junction on local passenger trains in the same way.

The Sanquhar traffic was arranged so that the tanks arrived in London at midday after leaving Scotland the previous evening, remaining overnight at Rossmore Road to return empty the next morning. Three loaded tanks were deposited at Verney Junction every morning at 8.31, were conveyed to Aylesbury on a train leaving at 8.50 and were then attached to the 10.33 Marylebone train. Coming back, empty tanks left Marylebone on a mail and passenger train departing at four in the morning, were detached at Quainton Road and taken forward to be handed over to the LMS at Verney Junction. On each round trip the Sanquhar tanks covered a total distance of over 700 miles, and the service offers a remarkable example of how the transport of milk had developed in the space of a few years. No doubt it was the successful working of this traffic which influenced the

decision to introduce a similar service at Dorrington.

The latter step appears to have been taken early in 1936, for it was then that an order for 10 six-wheel vehicles of the type in use at Sanquhar was placed with the Great Western Railway. Of 3,060 gallons capacity, these were equipped with the usual special springing and fully automatic brakes to allow high-speed working; they received running numbers 2567-2576 and were completed in June 1936. The date of their actual introduction into service is not known for certain, but can be assumed to have been very shortly after this. To observers they were extremely distinctive vehicles because of the striking way in which they were painted. Railway vehicles have always lent themselves to advertising, private-owner coal wagons being an excellent example, and with these milk tanks IMS made full use of the opportunity. On each tank side, painted in large white letters, were the words INDEPENDENT MILK SUPPLIES, and underneath this in only slightly smaller characters, GLASS LINED HYGIENIC MILK SERVICE. The lettering appeared on two different backgrounds, some of the tanks being turned out a deep navy blue and others an equally striking old gold; the latter colour was probably chosen as a means of proclaiming the company's pride in its best product, the special Gold Top milk. Unfortunately these attractive finishes were soon spoilt by the inevitable coating of grime, and the tanks have been described by most observers as either black or brown, these being the shades to which the original blue and gold were reduced after a short time in service, while the lettering gradually faded from sight. In well-worn condition the 'hygienic' tanks became largely indistinguishable from vehicles conveying oil or tar. A regular cleaning schedule would of course have helped matters, but the dairy would have been unlikely to have had either the facilities or the labour to carry out such work, and it is also probable that the tanks were operated on a schedule which left little time for cleaning operations, at least as far as the tank exteriors were concerned.

The use of tank wagons at Dorrington required no addition to the existing facilities beyond the installation of a long flexible filler pipe leading from the cooling tanks on the upper floor: the tanks normally arrived in small numbers, probably not more than two or three at a time, and the filler pipe was simply inserted into each in turn without the need for intermediate shunting.

To reach Marylebone the milk had to traverse Great Western and Great Central metals. Its most obvious route, after joining the Paddington line at Birmingham, would have been to continue along this on to the GC&GW Joint Line at Ashendon Junction and thence directly into Marylebone, but instead it was worked along the GWR main line no further than Banbury where it completely changed course, being handed over to the LNER which took it in a northeasterly direction up to Woodford; here a second reversal took place so that it could proceed along the Great Central main line into Marylebone. The reason for this somewhat complicated routing was that, as the original agreement with IMS had been concluded by the LNER, the railway chose to operate the service over as much of its system as possible so as to create the maximum revenue. As a result, the Dorrington milk became the only southbound traffic to work regularly in the Banbury-Woodford direction.

Over LNER metals the milk was at first worked in the same way as the Sanquhar traffic, namely by being attached to the rear of existing passenger trains. Reaching Banbury in the evening after an afternoon departure from Dorrington, the milk tanks were attached to the 8.12pm passenger train to Woodford, due at 8.34; this was one of the daily series of passenger trains which plied between Banbury and Woodford and which were known locally as the 'Banbury Motor'. It was also one of several such which were advertised as connecting for Marylebone at Woodford, arrival at the former being at 11.11pm after a departure from Woodford at 8.52, and it was to this train that the milk tanks were transferred on reaching Woodford. The 8.52pm Woodford-Marylebone stopping passenger train was a Woodford working of long standing, the engine returning from London on an early morning goods; by the time the milk service began to operate it is believed to have been regularly worked by 'B7' 4-6-0, a type well represented at Woodford during the mid-1930s. The 11.11pm also claimed the distinction of being the last main-line arrival of the day in Marylebone.

Empty tanks left the terminus at the rear of the 7.30pm departure for Woodford, a similar train to the one just described, and believed also to have been a 'B7' working, though in this instance a Neasden responsibility. Arrival at Woodford was at 10 o'clock, and as there was no convenient train to Banbury the tanks remained at Woodford overnight, being worked forward on the 7.45 'Banbury Motor' next morning.

Somewhat different arrangements were in force on Sundays, and it has proved impossible to find any evidence of loaded tanks being worked up to London on a passenger train as happened during the week, possibly because there were no conveniently-timed trains to make use of; it seems probable therefore that the milk was worked separately on Sundays, and if so this was a harbinger of later developments. A similar arrangement operated in connection with the Sanquhar milk, which on Sunday mornings worked

as a separate train between Marylebone and Verney Junction, empty tanks departing at 6.1 and the milk getting in at 10.14 with the same engine in charge.

Empty tanks for Dorrington left Marylebone on the 9am stopping passenger train to Leicester, and after a very leisurely run were detached at Woodford at 12.04pm, though this was not a regular working and operated only on an 'as required' basis as far as the milk tanks were concerned. The main empty tank working was the 6.40pm departure, another Leicester stopping train, which brought the tanks into Woodford at 9.20, where they remained overnight to go forward on the 7.45 'Banbury Motor' the next morning, the train thus conveying empty milk tanks every morning except Sundays. From the autumn of 1937 the 6.40pm also became an 'as required' empty milk working, and so it is probable that the staff at Marylebone arranged to despatch the empty tanks in one load either on the 9am or its evening counterpart.

The procedure for dealing with milk arrivals at Marylebone was always the same. Immediately the train came to rest at the platform the milk tanks were uncoupled by a shunter while the station pilot ran in behind and hooked on to the rear; the tanks were then drawn out under the Rossmore Road overbridge and beyond the platform end to where the lines diverged into the milk depot, whence they were propelled and placed in position. Here IMS staff were waiting to receive them, and directly they came to rest a workman climbed the metal ladder on each tank and removed the filler covers, inserting a long rod with which he stirred up the contents. A pipe from the dairy was then lowered into each of the tanks in turn and the milk pumped out; as at Dorrington, the installation was designed to deal with several tanks without the need for intermediate shunting. Once emptied, the tanks were washed out and then drawn clear, being placed in an adjacent siding to await their return journey to Dorrington. The siding was readily visible from the nearby passenger platforms, and the tanks must soon have become a familiar sight to the commuters.

Shunters and staff employed in the Marylebone passenger sidings in those days included Bill Mathews – always known as 'Old Bill' to distinguish him from his son of the same name who worked at Neasden – Alf Yerby, Bert Sampson, George Trainer, Jack Phillips, 'Doc' Lord and his son Jack. It was a well-known fact that none of these individuals ever needed to bring bottles of milk to work, as a plentiful supply was always faithfully provided by the IMS staff, and the same courtesy was extended to the enginemen in charge of the pilot.

The timetable arrangements described earlier are known to have been in force during the summer and autumn of 1937, and it is probable that they had operated from the time when the milk service was first introduced in the previous year. Towards the close of 1937 however, or early in the following year, a major reorganisation took place by which the whole service was worked separately, full and empty tanks having their own individual timetable between Banbury and Marylebone. The reasons for this important step are not known, but the fact that the loaded tanks were now arriving in Banbury much earlier in the afternoon indicates that the traffic was being dealt with more expeditiously at Dorrington, with a consequent need to rearrange the rail workings; arrival of the full tanks in Banbury at about 5.30pm instead of the previous 8pm meant that there was no convenient passenger train by which they could be conveyed to Woodford as there was no 'Banbury Motor' between 5pm and 8.12pm. Since delay to the loaded tanks was unacceptable in the interests of keeping the milk as fresh as possible, the LNER had no alternative but to arrange completely separate working. In order to operate this with the maximum economy a new diagram made its appearance in the GC section locomotive schedules, with Neasden engines and men working full and empty tanks as part of a single out-and-back roster. Thus did a milk train proper, as opposed to the working of milk tanks on passenger trains, become a daily feature of GC section traffic.

Leaving Marylebone at 2.09pm with empty tanks, the Neasden engine and men reached Woodford at 4.05, where they reversed and continued to Banbury for 4.50pm. Shortly after the GWR train arrived with the loaded milk, and after this had been handed over in the Banbury Junction reception sidings, the Neasden engine went back the way it had come, reversing at Woodford for the second time and reaching Marylebone at 8.20. The times were slightly different on Sundays, with the empties leaving Marylebone at 3.20pm and eventually reaching Banbury at 6pm; the return trip brought the loaded tanks into Marylebone at 9.43pm after departing from Banbury at 7.02. A further slight difference in the Sunday arrangements was that the down empties travelled via the GC&GW Joint Line through High Wycombe instead of taking the Aylesbury route as did all the other milk trains, and as had been the case in the days of passenger train working.

The milk trains quickly became familiar because of their unmistakeable make-up of three or sometimes four tanks together with a distinctive six-wheel van which contained a guard's compartment as well as having room for the conveyance of churns; the presence of this vehicle suggests that the output of milk at Dorrington had increased since the days of passenger working, when there were apparently no facilities for transporting churns except by the very laborious method of transhipping at Banbury and Woodford. An interesting feature of the double reversal at Woodford was that the allowance of 18 minutes in both directions was insufficient for the engine to turn at Woodford Loco, which meant tender-first running on both directions along the Woodford-Banbury section, and turning at Banbury Loco; on Sundays the allowance at Woodford was reduced to eight minutes, probably because the lighter Sunday traffic would allow the necessary manoeuvring to be carried out more quickly. The Sunday reversals were also carried out in a different location, at the Woodford North loop instead of Woodford itself; this was probably because of the closure of certain signalboxes during Sunday afternoons.

The earliest published report of the new-style milk trains indicates that they were being regularly worked by one of the well-tried Neasden 'Directors', No 5506 Butler-Henderson. This appeared in April 1938 together with some details of how the milk was worked over the GWR system[3], but the use of 'Director' class engines did not persist, as many other types were later noted. These included 'A5' or 'L1' tanks, 'B7' or 'J11' mixed traffic types, or 'C4' Atlantics – in short almost any kind of engine allocated to Neasden at that period except for pure shunting tanks. The advantages of using a tank engine on the milk were very obvious, namely the elimination of turning at Banbury and none of the discomforts of tender-first working between there and Woodford, but how often they were actually employed is not known; the Neasden 'A5s' were of course more than well occupied in running the frequent and well-patronised suburban services on the two routes out of Marylebone, but the large number of these engines on the allocation, virtually all the class, allowed for a spare one to be rostered for the milk on days when things were running smoothly. Hence nearly all of the class appeared on the milk at some time or other in the years up to the war, though only two specific dates have been traced – No 5452 on Wednesday 31 May 1939 and No 5006 on Thursday 4 July. Compared with their normal work, the Dorrington milk was probably the most unusual the 'A5s' were ever put in charge of, and certainly a very far cry from the task for which they had been designed; it also involved the furthest distance from Marylebone which they ever worked in ordinary service, Brackley being the most northerly station they reached on suburban passenger trains. It is unlikely that they were much used on the milk turn at weekends, as Saturday was always likely to be a day of heavy demand on the local services, and there were often specials to be worked to Wembley Stadium in connection with various events staged there, while Sunday was 'shed day' for most of the class; this probably explains why most photographs of the Dorrington milk show tender engines in charge.

By comparison with the large fleet of 'A5s', Neasden's allocation of 'L1' tanks was very small indeed, consisting in January 1938 of Nos 5339, 5342 and 5344, to which a further engine, No 5340, was added during that month. All are remembered as having appeared on the milk train at some time prior to the war, but no exact dates have survived. Like the 'A5s', they were no doubt popular on the working because of the better protection afforded on the Woodford-Banbury section, and the elimination of turning meant that the crew could enjoy a very welcome break during the 50-minute wait at Banbury.

The use of tank engines on a round trip totalling over 160 miles meant that some provision had to be made for taking water en route, and stops for this purpose were a regular part of the milk schedule – at Aylesbury on the outward trip, and Great Missenden coming back. Coal presented no difficulty as both 'A5s' and 'L1s' had a bunker capacity in excess of four tons, an ample supply for the distance involved.

The regular working of No 5506 *Butler-Henderson* on the milk train early in 1938 is a reminder of the fact that the 'D11' 'Directors' were one of the most popular classes on the GC section, and although No 5506 was transferred away from Neasden during the summer other members of the class appeared on the Dorrington turn from time to time, as for instance on Sunday 28 May 1939 when No 5510 *Princess Mary* was in charge. However, such things should not be allowed to obscure the fact that the use of 'Directors' on such a train can hardly be regarded as anything other than a notable example of downgrading, for although the milk was operated on a smart schedule between Marylebone and Woodford it cannot be said to have presented much of a problem for a 'Director'; the days when these proud engines had been the mainstay of Neasden's passenger fleet were finished, and now it was becoming a case of finding them some convenient job which they could comfortably work.

Something similar could also be said for the 'B7' 4-6-0s, which for years had monopolised the long-distance fast goods workings on the GC section and been first choice for the heavy passenger specials and excursions at weekends.

Just as the 'Directors' had been forced to give way to more modern LNER-built types, they too were being increasingly ousted by similar rivals, in particular Class K3 engines. How often the 'B7s' were used on the Dorrington milk is not known, and the only note which has survived shows No 5468 working the turn on Thursday 15 June 1939, but it is certain that only a few short years before such a job would have been well below their dignity; nor can they have been regarded as a particularly suitable choice, as their considerable power was obviously much under-utilised on such a lightweight train.

Cast more for the role were the 'J11' 'Pom-poms', which among many other duties specialised in the sort of light, fast working which the Dorrington Milk offered. Furthermore they were as popular an engine from the men's point of view as one could find anywhere on the GC system. However Neasden's allocation of 'J11s' was never very large, and it was not a shed at which members of the class settled down for any great length of time; No 5282, noted working the Dorrington Milk on Friday 26 May 1939, was to leave Neasden a few weeks after the outbreak of war, having been there only since the spring of 1936.

A word may also be said about the GWR engines used. Here a certain contrast was to be observed, for it seems to have been GWR policy to roster the same engine types for the milk turn, rather than offering the kind of variety which has just been described, and this was particularly the case after the arrival of 'Manor' class engines in 1938. Originally the turn was worked by 4-4-0 passenger types, and two 'Bulldog' class engines are especially remembered – Nos 3442 *Bullfinch* and 3445 *Flamingo*; there is also a photograph showing the train being worked by one of the very similar 'Earl' class 4-4-0s, No 3224. Like the LNER 'D11s' these engines had of course seen better days on fast passenger workings, but were now reduced to filling in on lightweight jobs as their original duties were taken over by more modern types. The introduction of the 'Manor' class 4-6-0s in 1938 soon had its effect on the Dorrington service however, for in May of that year two examples of the new type were put to work on it – Nos 7805 *Broome Manor* and 7806 *Cockington Manor*. This pair quickly settled down to a consistent pattern of working, appearing on alternate days right up to the start of the war, and possibly for some time after that. GWR footplatemen referred to the turn as the 'Milky', whereas the LNER staff appear to have stuck to the official name of 'Dorrington Milk'.

For the LNER footplatemen the job fitted neatly into the confines of an eight-hour shift, with an allowance of time either for engine preparation beforehand or disposal after completing the trip. Unfortunately no light engine departure time from Neasden Loco appears in the working timetables, but to be ready for the starting-time of 2.09pm the engine would have been leaving Neasden by 1.45 at the very latest, which gives an approximate booking-on time of 12.45 if engine preparation was included in the diagram, though it is possible that the engine was remanned after working another job beforehand – such practices were the rule rather than the exception on the LNER by 1938. Return arrival in Marylebone at 8.20pm would have enabled the crew to book off by about 8.45 provided no disposal work was involved – such chores varied on different diagrams, depending on the length of time left to make up the full shift after the crew had got back to the shed.

The men allotted to the milk job are believed to have come from the very prestigious Pipe Train Link, so called because most of the work involved fitted goods trains. Membership of the link entailed frequent night shifts and the performance of heavy and exacting work in accordance with a strict time-schedule; there was also some lodging to be done, including a turn to Manchester. On all these counts the Dorrington job, with its straightforward Banbury-and-back schedule carried out at a convenient time of day with a lightweight load, formed a welcome break from routine. It is doubtful if the regular roster would include the Sunday working, as the hard-working Pipe Train men were usually allowed to treat the Sabbath as a genuine day of rest, which they probably needed after lodging overnight at Gorton, for example; the odd working is more likely to have been manned on a casual basis, either by crews who needed to refresh their knowledge of the High Wycombe line, or by those who had been lucky enough to enjoy a recent sequence of free Sundays; failing these, there were always a few crews eager to put a few extra shillings in their pockets for the sake of turning out on a Sunday afternoon. At about the time when the Dorrington turn was introduced, Drivers Jack Proctor and Jack Fisher are known to have been in the Pipe Train Link, but they were fairly soon promoted into the Top Link and the identities of their replacements are not known.

Guards worked a diagram largely identical to the footplatemen, changing at Banbury from the outward-bound van to its opposite number on the incoming train. All were Marylebone-based, and came from one of the passenger train links: they included Frank Chorlton, Mark Swain and Stan Peplow.

Besides its unusual route, the Dorrington milk was unique in several ways as far as GC section trains are concerned. It was for instance the only non-passenger train to be fairly regularly worked by engines such as the 'D11' Directors. It was the only self-contained milk train to run on a daily schedule over the GC section, and ranked as one of the shortest non-passenger trains operating regularly. In many ways it presented a marked contrast to the kind of traffics traditionally associated with the GCR, which were chiefly associated with heavy industry in some form or other: in this respect it was linked directly with the growth of the new light industries which social historians have identified as emerging in certain areas of outer London during the interwar years, just as the established GCR mineral traffics were associated with the declining north. No doubt it provided a useful source of revenue on the somewhat under-utilised section of line south of Woodford, but the very light nature of the load did not lend itself to economical use of the locomotives. 'Full train loads' had become something of a watchword among railway traffic officers at that period, and in this respect the Dorrington milk clearly fell a long way below the optimum. Although a high-value commodity compared with such traffics as coal, the quantities of milk transported were of course strictly limited by the factors of supply and demand. However, in spite of these things the Dorrington milk soldiered on into the war years, and unlike many Great Central traffics survived it and continued into the BR era.

Notes
1 Iolo A. Williams, *The Firm of Cadbury*.
2 *Great Central Railway Journal*, April 1907.
3 *RCTS Railway Observer*, April 1938.

Top:
A spick and span combination at Southam Road & Harbury station in 1937 as an unidentified GWR 'Mogul' heads for Banbury with the Dorrington milk, taking precedence over a goods train in the background.
Photo G. Coltas

Above:
GWR 'Mogul' No 5324 is seen near Lapworth, south of Birmingham, with the Dorrington milk on 19 June 1936.
Photo C. F. H. Oldham

Top right:
'A5' No 5374 put in some appearances on the Dorrington

milk. It is seen here on a Marylebone suburban train at Chorley Wood & Chenies station in the late 1930s.**
Photo B. K. Cooper

Centre right:
'D11' No 5504 *Jutland* on down milk empties at Harrow-on-the-Hill about 1938; the grimy condition of the tanks will be noted.   *Photo C. R. L. Coles*

Right:
Postwar view at Marylebone with 'C13' No 67420 entering on a train from West Ruislip. IMS tank wagon and crates of bottled milk are visible in the right background.   *Photo K. A. C. R. Nunn*

VI

The New Frodingham

'. . . the extent of the town's growth is illustrated by the fact that, although thirty years ago the urban district population was only 10,000, today it exceeds 30,000; yet on the Frodingham iron and steel district, which is the area of the outcrop of the ironstone deposits, the prosperity of the whole surrounding urban district depends. As an individual station Frodingham & Scunthorpe takes the lead in the Southern Area of the LNER for handling the largest tonnage.'

LNER Magazine, December 1927

Apart from those particularly conversant with the LNER system, it is unlikely that Frodingham in North Lincolnshire was ever much more than a name to people not resident in the immediate vicinity. It qualifies for inclusion in this book by virtue of the fact that, in spite of its out-of-the-way location, it was the scene of one of the LNER's most costly and comprehensive schemes of reconstruction, involving the building of new passenger and goods stations, conversion of a derelict industrial site into a brand-new and up-to-date locomotive shed, and construction of a huge complex of yards and sidings, involving much attendent bridging work as well as re-alignment of the main Doncaster-Grimsby line.

As for the driving force behind this immense undertaking, it could be summed up in one word – steel. As a centre of the iron and steel industry Frodingham offered extremely favourable conditions: the local ironstone was easily won, and the excellent rail facilities ensured ample supplies of the necessary fuel from the Yorkshire and Nottinghamshire coalfields besides facilitating the transport of finished products; progressive management played an important part, and the success story was completed by the huge increase in demand that was created before and during the Great War. By 1923 there were four major steel-making concerns in the district – John Lysaght's, Firth Brown's, Richard Thomas, and the United Steel Co, the last named having separate plants at Appleby and Frodingham.

All materials were moved by rail. Inward traffic consisted of coal, coke, ironstone, lime, limestone and refractory bricks, while in the opposite direction went pig iron, steel billets, sheetbar, ingots, sections and so on, as well as the locally mined ironstone despatched to the blast furnaces at such places as Staveley, Sheepbridge, Parkgate and Ardsley. All these traffics were worked round the clock, and with a further growth in steel production during the 1930s the reader will perhaps understand something of the importance of Frodingham as a railway centre.

Unfortunately the facilities inherited by the LNER had been considerably outstripped by the rate of expansion in the local trade, and even allowing for some drop in production after the war, still fell far short of what was needed. In January 1923 the layout at Frodingham followed the east-west axis of the Doncaster-Grimsby main line, which was joined on its northern side by the North Lindsey Light Railway, the junction being in the form of an eastward-facing curve. Two yards of very modest size, known as Trent Yard and Old Appleby Sidings, were located on the south side of the main line east of the junction, the latter accessible by a short spur usually referred to as the North Lincoln branch, which also led to some blast furnaces nearby. These yards had respective capacities of 1,500 and 500 wagons and, together with a few sidings at the junction with the North Lindsey Railway, they formed the sum total of the shunting and standage space available for the whole of the Frodingham complex, apart from the works at Normanby Park which had its own separate sidings on the North Lindsey line, capable of taking 800 wagons. The most serious problem with the Normanby Park sidings was that all its traffic had to be brought on to and off the main line via the east-facing curve at the junction, which meant that trains working to or from the west had to be reversed.

The extent to which railway investment had lagged behind can best be judged from the fact that the meagre facilities were for the most part of quite recent vintage, and their generally unsatisfactory nature was the result of a lack of any co-ordinated plan, the various sidings having been constructed on a piecemeal basis as the need arose. Thus for example two separate extensions to the main sidings had been put in, one in 1912 and the other in 1921, while the North Lindsey Railway itself was a comparative newcomer to the scene, having been opened only in 1905. The decision to link it with the main line by means of an eastward curve was probably the result of a desire to achieve through communication with the proposed Blyton &

odingham Light Railway; the latter project
oved abortive but the east curve was put in as
anned, and instead of being a benefit to the new
stallation it turned into a serious hindrance once
e works at Normanby Park opened a few years
ter.
  As an indication of the volume of work that took
ace, the working timetable of 1924 gives no
wer than seven pilot engines, two at Normanby
rk sidings and the rest operating in the vicinity
the main line, all save two working right round
e clock. In addition to these there was a separate
lot stationed at Keadby, six miles to the west,
quired for banking eastbound trains up the climb
to Frodingham.
Growth of steel production had naturally
oduced growth of the township itself, and this
d also worked to the disadvantage of the existing
ilway facilities. The passenger station, somewhat
ortentously named Frodingham & Scunthorpe,
s located in the original Frodingham settlement,
d by 1923 was completely surrounded by blast
rnaces and belching chimneys. A further
oblem created by the population growth was the
creasing burden on the station's goods facilities:
liveries of all classes of goods and foodstuffs into
e district, and in particular the unloading and
ansporting of supplies of domestic coal, all
creased in proportion.

---

he solution to all the various problems, clearly,
as to undertake a complete reconstruction of the
dings and other facilities to cater properly for the
rious traffics. It is believed that the GCR had
riously considered a radical scheme of
provement as early as 1907, but this had come to
ught after an attempt to purchase land
rthwest of the passenger station had failed
cause of difficulties with the landowners, the
esence of ironstone deposits evidently pushing
e price beyond what the Great Central was
epared to pay. So it was left to the LNER to
ckle the situation, setting to work almost at once
draw up an ambitious scheme of improvements.
The LNER has been frequently described in
ilway literature as a company which seldom
ent money freely, and while this may be true in
rtain respects it is a view which tends to overlook
e truly enormous expenditures undertaken in the
ld of civil engineering. According to a local
wspaper, the cost of improvements carried out
Frodingham up to 1928, when the work still had
veral years to run, amounted to £300,000, and by
at date work was already well advanced on
other similar project at Whitemoor, while
rther extensive works were to follow at
ottram, and in the building of the new fish dock

at Grimsby. The huge cost of the Frodingham
scheme can perhaps be better understood by a
consideration of the various tasks involved, which
may be summarised as follows:

a. Diversion of the Doncaster-Grimsby main line
   for a distance of over one mile.
b. Provision of an extensive network of sidings to
   form a new yard capable of taking
   approximately 1,600 wagons.
c. Construction of a new goods depot.
d. Laying in a west curve to match the existing east
   curve from the main line to the North Lindsey
   Light Railway.
e. Building of an entirely new passenger station on
   a fresh site.
f. Construction of a locomotive running shed
   together with all attendant facilities.
g. A complete programme of re-signalling
   entailing erection of two new cabins.

In total it was estimated that 11 miles of sidings
and 2½ miles of running lines would be required to
complete the trackwork.
  Parliamentary approval for the scheme was
given about 1925, ironically at a time when most of
the country's heavy industries were already well
into a period of unrelieved depression. Once the
postwar boom began to collapse about 1921, the
local furnaces were soon forced to operate at well
below capacity, and this led in 1924 to the closure
of the Richard Thomas works at Redbourn, the
most recent of Frodingham's steel plants. Full
production was not resumed there until 1933,
thereafter the works operated continuously.
  Early victim of the depression though it was
Redbourn owed its closure partly to the vexed
question of railway rates. The company's chairman
stated clearly at the time that the cost of conveying
most of the firm's steel output to the Swansea area
of South Wales had proved prohibitively high. This
situation affords an illuminating contrast with that
of the John Lysaght works at Normanby Park,
which had been able to negotiate specially
favourable rates with the GCR as a result of the
promised enhancement of traffic following its
arrival on a 'green field' site in 1912. Lysaght's also
had the advantage that the company's steel output
was bound for Newport, as opposed to the more
distant Swansea.
  Another victim of the times, though small by
comparison, was the passenger service which
operated on the North Lindsey Light Railway.
Linking Frodingham with the remote village of
Whitton, some 10 miles away on the bank of the
River Humber, this service had never amounted to
very much since its opening in the early years of
the century, and by Grouping it was down to one
train a day in each direction. Working into its own

separate terminus close to the GCR line, the North Lindsey passenger service was very much a self-contained affair, the station being at right angles to the larger system and proudly named Scunthorpe to distinguish it from the nearby main-line station already described. Activity here finally ceased on Saturday 25 July 1925.

It was against a seemingly unpromising background therefore that the mechanical excavators and their attendant gangs of navvies arrived in Frodingham towards the end of 1926. However, gloomy though this period may appear when seen through the writings of historians and economists, it would be a mistake to assume that the LNER directors and management were anything other than optimistic. During 1925, some 18 months before the work began, the government had taken the fateful step of putting Britain back on the Gold Standard – an act of faith in the country's future which held out a message of hope and encouragement to all concerned in trade, for the Gold Standard had long been regarded as the supreme symbol of Britain's financial and industrial pre-eminence. With the advantage of hindsight we know now that the return to the Gold Standard realised none of the benefits that were claimed for it, but at the time it was regarded by many as a kind of symbolic end to the industrial difficulties which were widely attributed to the after-effects of the Great War.

In order to minimise interference with rail traffic the works were planned in stages, with the new west curve to the North Lindsey Railway being put in first, followed by excavation of land on either side of the main line to form the site of the new yard, this being in some respects the principal feature of the whole development. Levelling work on the down side was completed first and the line was then switched to that location so as to leave the way well clear for the remaining excavations, the new alignment being permanent. Spoil removed from the area of the new yard was tipped to level off the site of the enlarged goods station, and also to form the embankment of the soon-to-be-diverted Scunthorpe-Brigg main road. Reconstruction of the roadways was an important feature of the scheme, and involved the provision of two overbridges, one on Ashby Road replacing an existing single-arch bridge spanning the two tracks of the original main line, and the Brigg Road bridge taking the place of a level crossing lying immediately east of the old main-line passenger station; the latter involved diversion of the road over a distance of about half of mile and construction of substantial embankments on either side of the line. The Ashby Road reconstruction was carried out first, a portion of the new bridge being built alongside the existing one before the latter was demolished; traffic was then transferred

on to the new portion while the old bridge wa destroyed by means of explosives, this task bein carried out on Sunday 17 July 1927. The Brig; Road scheme took somewhat longer to complet because of the work involved in building the larg embankments. Both bridges were of considerabl size, the one at Ashby Road being long enough t span the western approach roads to the new yar as well as the repositioned main line, while th 400ft long Brigg Road bridge could perhaps b better described as a viaduct. Both structures wer wide enough to allow an ample carriageway with pedestrian footpaths on either side.

Construction of the new west curve on to th North Lindsey line involved certain changes at th former passenger terminus. The single platform now disused, was demolished, while the statio buildings were retained for the use of the ne goods office staff; a single-road corrugated iro shed which in former times had housed the stoc for the now defunct passenger service wa dismantled in order to clear the way for the ne curve.

As some buildings were demolished, other sprang up. A new goods warehouse lying directl astride the old Brigg Road was scheduled to go u directly the new road was open, and in th meantime work went vigorously ahead o construction of the new passenger station. Locate a short distance east of the Ashby Road bridge and opposite a point where the new road branched out from the goods line into the yard, i was a straightforward design of wayside statio with platform faces on the up and down lines, an bays at each end of the north platform; th buildings were mainly brick, and of a particularl neat and simple construction. It was brought int operation on Sunday 11 March 1928, the last stage of the work being carried out in weather condition typical of that time of year. The contractors Messrs Caffin & Co of London, had worked righ through the Saturday night and early Sunda morning in continuous snow in order to have th station ready for the big occasion, the main tas being to remove the up platform of the ol Frodingham & Scunthorpe station and to lay in th final connections with the new route.

The first train to use the station was the 9.05ar New Holland-Penistone stopping passenger, an its arrival at 10.15 prompted a modest ceremony District railway officials, local councillors and th contractors' agent stood by as a certain Mrs Jones a clerk at the nearby Wortley Hotel, boarded th engine in company with her colleague Mrs Jeffre and started the train off on the next stage of it journey. Newspaper accounts of the event var slightly, one paper stating that Mrs Jones did n more than open the regulator, another that sh actually drove the train out of the station. One c he papers described the ceremony as 'a quiet opening in wintry weather', and in some respects the comparative absence of publicity is curious, as by this date the LNER had shown itself to be a company very well aware of the virtues of advertising. The local corporation had written to the LNER a month previously to ask whether it planned to stage a civic ceremony, and the company's failure to take up the idea seems very un-characteristic.

No such reticence was to be noted when it came to the opening of the Brigg Road bridge and diversion on Thursday 28 June. A huge gathering of civic leaders and other dignitaries were on hand to see the ceremonial ribbon cut by one of Lincolnshire's most distinguished sons, Field-Marshal Sir William Robertson, who in a rare career had risen from the ranks to the very top of his profession, becoming Chief of the Imperial General Staff during the Great War. He was accompanied by a well-known local figure, Sir Berkeley Sheffield of nearby Normanby Hall, formerly a director of the Great Central Railway, and both were presented with specially-made walking sticks to mark the occasion.

It is not possible to give a precise date for the opening of the new yard as the various roads were simply brought into use in stages directly the trackwork could be laid. With Redbourn coming back into production during 1928, traffic was on the increase, and every new length of line that could be put down was speedily brought into use. With this installation complete, and matched by a newly opened passenger station in a pleasant part of the town, together with a modern overbridge in place of the troublesome Brigg Road level crossing, the LNER could boast that from a railway traffic point of view Frodingham had at last reached the 20th century. It was now time to turn to the locomotive side of things.

Bearing in mind the primitive state of the Frodingham yards at Grouping, the reader will hardly be surprised to learn that the locomotive arrangements were equally out of date. A single-road shed large enough to take two engines was the sum total of covered accommodation available in the district, and the shortage of buildings was such that an old van body had been pressed into service as a store, while two defunct coachholders officiated as workshops – referred to as 'the dug-outs' by Sir Sam Fay in the course of a tour of inspection during the Great War. Repair work was carried out in the open, with easily imagined discomforts in freezing weather, and the only concession to modernity was a long inspection pit that had been installed after the first large

superheated engines had gone into service. The location of this antiquated establishment was also far from ideal, as contrary to what has been said in at least one history of the GCR[1], it was situated some distance away from Frodingham. Its location at Keadby, over six miles west of the original Frodingham & Scunthorpe station, meant that every job which started and finished at the steelworks involved more than 12 miles of unproductive light engine running. Furthermore each inward journey involved an ascent of the long gradient on the east bank of the Trent, where it was easy to aggravate congestion among the procession of mineral trains toiling up the grade. Further problems were created by the two intervening bridges, the South Yorkshire Navigation bridge and the well-known Scherzer bridge over the River Trent, both frequently opened for river traffic, and imposing unavoidable delays. The most serious difficulties were encountered in hot weather when the girderwork on the big Scherzer bridge expanded while it was in the open position, preventing it from returning to the horizontal. When this happened a slightly Chaplinesque remedy had to be resorted to whereby the local fire brigade were called out to hose the bridge down, with severe curtailment of rail activity in the meantime. In 1926 the original steam-driven swing bridge over the adjacent canal was replaced by a modern electric drawbridge, but this still had to be opened for the passage of barges.

The catalogue of drawbacks afflicting Keadby Loco continues with the question of water. All locomotive requirements were met by drawing from the South Yorkshire Canal running directly alongside, but as the water at this point mixed with the tidal River Trent it was hardly suitable for locomotive boilers. In those days the village of Keadby, a typical settlement of rural Lincolnshire, had no mains water supply, and most householders made use of rainwater butts. When, as sometimes happened, word got round that a Sheffield engine was standing on the shed, railwaymen's families would arrive on the scene armed with buckets and other receptacles which they would fill from the engine's tender, Pennine water having an excellent reputation in this part of the world.

The ancient turntable was a much overdue for replacement as everything else at Keadby, being only 43ft 7in long and therefore too short to turn the eight-coupled mineral engines that were the mainstay of the shed's allocation. A 'Pom-Pom' 0-6-0 could just be accommodated, but could only be turned in one direction or else the front of the engine would foul the adjacent blacksmith's shop. The turntable was extremely stiff to operate, and with an engine in position it often required the combined efforts of several of the staff to get it

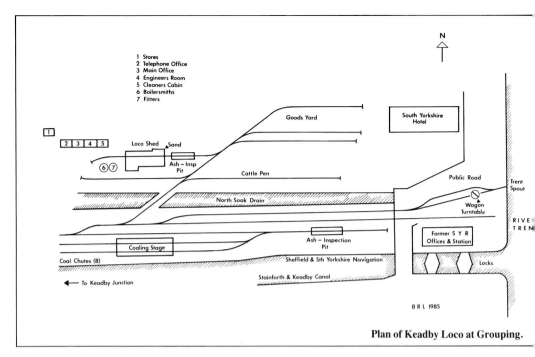

1 Stores
2 Telephone Office
3 Main Office
4 Engineers Room
5 Cleaners Cabin
6 Boilersmiths
7 Fitters

N

Goods Yard

South Yorkshire
Hotel

1

2 3 4 5   Loco Shed   Sand

6 7   Ash – Insp
Pit

Cattle Pen

Public Road

Trent
Spout

North Soak Drain

Wagon
Turntable

RIVE
TREN

Former S Y R
Offices & Station

Ash – Inspection
Pit

Coaling Stage

Coal Chutes (8)   Sheffield & Sth Yorkshire Navigation   Locks

← To Keadby Junction   Stainforth & Keadby Canal

B R L 1985

Plan of Keadby Loco at Grouping.

moving. Yet another drawback was the position of the turntable on the opposite side of the main line, which meant that all engines had to make two crossings of the line whenever it was necessary to turn. Long mineral engines had to be turned in Frodingham, originally on the triangle at what was known as North Lincoln Junction, or later on the angle of lines formed by the new curve to the North Lindsey Railway.

The coaling-stage was yet another incredibly primitive affair, built of rough timbers and with a rudimentary roof which gave little or no protection from the elements; complete absence of any modern equipment meant that coal had to be shovelled direct from wagons onto the locomotives.

The absurdly small size of the shed building meant that, for all practical purposes, the entire allocation had to be stabled permanently in the open, and in this respect also Keadby was wanting, because of limited yard space. At weekends it was usual for an influx of visiting engines to be parked at the shed, and in order to accommodate these birds of passage it was necessary to clear certain sidings adjacent to the canal on which loaded coal wagons normally stood during the week. These were shunted to a siding on the other side of Keadby Junction and then brought back into position when the engines went back to work during Sunday night.

Since Keadby was classed as a sub-shed of Mexborough in GCR days the details of its allocation at Grouping are somewhat vague, as it

was the practice to transfer engines to and from th parent depot without any record being show Classes 'J10' and 'J12', locally known as 'Claddi and 'Jumbos', are believed to have predominate though slowly giving way to more powerful 0-6 and 0-8-0 engines of Robinson design. F shunting duties there were a number of the ancie saddle tanks known as 'Humpies', officially Cla J59, supplemented by some 0-6-2 tanks of Class l or N5. Because of limited watering facilities t tank engines were more or less confined to t immediate vicinity of Keadby, although t situation was remedied in 1926 when the LNE authorised the installation of a parachute-ty water column and small wooden coaling-sta adjacent to the new west curve of the Nor Lindsey line. The Keadby tank engines h sometimes been used on the short-lived Nor Lindsey passenger service, and for many years t remained the only daily passenger worki performed by local engines, apart from a morni workmen's train ex-Thorne.

The heavier work associated with Frodingha was thus undertaken by the 0-8-0s and 0-6-0s, the jobs including the pilot and trip workings in t vicinity of the yards as well as main-line turns. 1924 a few Class O4 2-8-0s began to arrive Keadby, no doubt as a result of the purchase the LNER of a batch of surplus War Departme engines of the same type. As at most other form GCR sheds, main-line work at Keadby involv plenty of lodging, the usual venues bei Mexborough, Sheffield, Staveley, Ardsley a

96

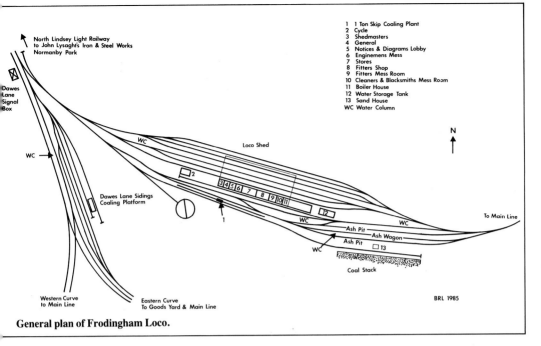

1 1 Ton Skip Coaling Plant
2 Cycle
3 Shedmasters
4 General
5 Notices & Diagrams Lobby
6 Enginemens Mess
7 Stores
8 Fitters Shop
9 Fitters Mess Room
10 Cleaners & Blacksmiths Mess Room
11 Boiler House
12 Water Storage Tank
13 Sand House
WC Water Column

General plan of Frodingham Loco.

Lincoln. Visiting enginemen lodged in the same way, though as there was only limited accommodation in the small village of Keadby they usually found a bed on Queen Street in Frodingham.

The reconstruction works at Frodingham were not without their effect on the locomotive situation at Keadby, the most notable development being the allocation of Class J50 tank engines from November 1927. Adopted as a standard type by the LNER, these GNR-designed machines became widely known during the Grouping era, being sent to many different parts of the LNER. The original five engines of 1927, Nos 1069, 1079, 1082, 1086 and 3225, were joined by Nos 610 and 1063 during 1928, and later on came Nos 1058, 1074 and 1081. Built by the LNER to the original pre-Grouping design, they were the most modern engines allocated in the district at the time, and must have stood out all the more by reason of their unmistakeable Great Northern lineaments, so different from the native GCR types.

The growing total of 'J50s' points to the demand for more engines as new portions of the layout were brought into use. The choice of 'J50s' probably reflected the desire to increase the weight of trip train loads between the various yards, as these engines were of considerably greater power than the 'J10s' which are believed to have been used on this work previously. Such a concentration of power into a tiny package made the 'J50s' ideal machines for the kind of work that Frodingham had to offer, and it is hardly surprising that the

class were still well represented there when World War 2 began.

During 1929-31 some rather unusual tank engines appeared in the district in the shape of a heavy 0-6-4 of Class M1, a Class J63 0-6-0, and two of the 'L1' 'Crab' 2-6-4s. It is believed that the large engines were sent to Keadby to be tried on work that was too heavy for the 'J50s', while the diminutive 'J63', total length only 27ft, may have been tried in the vicinity of Keadby itself, where there were some tight curves and other awkward locations. The 'M1' was No 6147, noted during the week beginning 10 February 1930, while 'J63' No 5157 appeared early in the following June; the 'Crabs', Nos 5273 and 5369, had come on the scene much earlier, in June 1929. Only these two were officially shown as moving to Keadby, the others being presumably sent on loan; according to the current records, No 5157 was at Liverpool and the 'M1' on the LDEC, where the class spent virtually its entire life. Nothing more was heard of the two latter classes after these appearances, but the 'Crabs' appear to have made their mark, as although they were transferred away within a few months, further members of the class arrived in the district soon after the new shed had opened in 1932.

Work on the construction of the new establishment appears to have begun towards the end of 1930. The new site, formerly the property of the Lindsey Iron Co, lay on the up side of the Doncaster-Grimsby line near the extended goods depot, and northeast of the newly-built triangle onto the North Lindsey line. The land had been extensively excavated in the days of ironstone mining, which meant that all structures had to have foundations down to a depth of 20ft, and with this in mind the LNER opted for a rather smaller building than had been originally envisaged, leaving room for later extensions if the traffic was found to justify it; the same factor may have had some bearing on the Great Central's earlier decision not to proceed with its own scheme.

Completed at the beginning of June 1932, the new shed was generously spread out on an ample site, dominated by a distinctive five-road double-ended building made of the same reinforced concrete as the nearby road bridges. It was in every way a notable advance on the facilities at Keadby, with covered accommodation for 20 engines as well as provision for extensions, and such modern conveniences as a wheel drop and roller-blind doors. Perhaps the greatest improvement of all was its location, for the yards, sidings and passenger station were all situated within a highly convenient radius.

The only facility which appeared to be in any way skimped was the mechanical coaling plant, which took the form of a small Mitchell conveyor, as used in the locomotive yard at Kings Cross station. This was clearly inadequate for a shed the size of Frodingham, and probably represented an attempt to economise on construction costs; it was replaced by a more suitable coaling hopper of the usual LNER style in 1938. The coaling stage at the North Lindsey triangle was retained for emergency use, and in fact survived to the end of steam.

Similar afterthoughts occurred in connection with the water supply. Because of the unsatisfactory local water the LNER had contracted to obtain a better quality supply from the boreholes of a nearby firm, the North Lincolnshire Iron Co, but this soon proved to be too hard, and failed to bring about the anticipated economies in boiler and firebox maintenance. As a result of this a chemical treatment plant was installed at the east end of the shed in 1935 and realised a considerable improvement, although even after this the water at Frodingham was never regarded as particularly good.

With the arrival of the 'J50s' and other fairly modern engines the local allocation had improved considerably from the miserable collection of early LNER days, and when the new shed was finally brought into use the engines sent there included representatives of Classes O4, Q4, J11 and J50, as well as 'Y3' Sentinel engine of very recent construction. The venerable 'Bulldogs' and 'Humpies', properly called Classes J12 and J59, had by this time become extinct after many years service in the district, and the 'J10' engines had also vanished from the local scene.

The move to Frodingham took place on Sunday 12 June 1932, and so far as is known it took place without any ceremony. The apparent desire to avoid publicity, so uncharacteristic of the LNER has already been remarked on, and contrast rather strangely with the opening of Thornton Junction shed in the Scottish area not very long afterwards, which took place to the accompaniment of a ceremony attended by the company Chairman and several other notables.

Apart from two short articles about the loco shed in the *LNER Magazine*, and a longer one in the *Railway Engineer* covering the yards published references to the area are few. During the entire reconstruction programme there was only one event which could be described as in any way unusual, this being the visit of 'B3' No 6167 in the afternoon of Tuesday 1 December 1931 to test the new Ransomes & Rapier turntable. Resplendent in passenger green, this engine was sent from Immingham specially for the purpose, running light in both directions.

Keadby Loco was completely closed on the day that Frodingham opened, and from then on the only resident railway activity at Keadby was that associated with the three pilots, the engines for these duties being sent daily from Frodingham. Apart from the No 2 Pilot, which was responsible for banking goods and mineral trains up the gradient into Frodingham, these were employed mainly in tasks connected with the local shipment of coal. The No 1 Pilot spent a good part of its time in the sidings at Keadby Canal Junction, shunting wagons of coal for shipment in vessels on the canal and the River Trent, as well as taking traffic in and out of various works sidings on both sides of the river. A 'J11' 'Pom-Pom' was usually placed on this duty. One of the main tasks of the No 3 Pilot was to work traffic at what was known locally as the Trent Spout, this being a device on the river bank by which wagons could be tilted bodily so as to discharge coal into waiting vessels: the wagons were placed in position by the pilot and then cable-hauled one by one up a small timber stage to the tipper. Only end-door wagons could be used, and a very necessary task in the preparation of traffic for the Trent Spout was to ensure that all wagons faced the right way; incoming trains were broken at Canal Junction for this purpose, and the No 3 Pilot was responsible for turning wagons was necessary, a turntable being provided in the sidings. The pilot also worked at the Canal coal drops, where coal was loaded into barges, and between spells of working on this and the Trent Spout traffic it was employed in shunting the goods yard behind the South Yorkshire public house. The No 3 Pilot job was usually in the care of the Frodingham Sentinel, which came down light from the shed at about 10 o'clock every morning.

To gain an understanding of the complicated network of yards and sidings at Frodingham, the reader is referred to the accompanying plan showing the location of the main yards and the various works. Incoming traffic from the west, which formed the bulk of the arrivals in Frodingham, was routed into what were known as the Group A sidings in the newly-built yard, where the trains were then sorted in preparation for dispatch to the works. These reception sidings occupied about two-thirds of the roads in the New Yard, as it soon became known, and were very much at the centre of the improvements brought about by the reconstruction scheme. Virtually all trains working into Frodingham were mixed – or 'rough', to use the word favoured by the staff – and the reception portion of the New Yard therefore acted as a filter for much of the inward traffic, relieving the pressure on the other yards. A large proportion of the incoming traffic consisted of coal, mostly from the south Yorkshire collieries via Wath Yard; these trains were made up of consignments for the various works which in turn originated from a variety of pits, the coal owners of course all having their own separate contracts with the different steel companies. The task of sorting trains such as these took up a good many of the man-hours expended in the New Yard. Empty wagons associated with the finished steel traffic also arrived in Group A, and though sometimes rough-marshalled at Stainforth, some 16 miles to the west, invariably required resorting before being sent forward to the works.

The other part of the New Yard, Group B, was an assembly point for outgoing traffic, receiving a flow of trip workings from the various works and marshalling these for final departure. Two pilot engines were based more or less permanently at the New Yard, occupied in the assembly of both inward and outwards trains as well as assisting in the job of transferring the traffic forward to the works. The yard was shunted from the west end, and entry and exit to and from the main line were controlled by two new signalboxes, the westerly one named Scunthorpe and Frodingham, and the other Yard No 1. All shunting was done on the flat, and the work was therefore considerably slower than in a hump yard such as Whitemoor.

To the east of the New Yard lay the original yards, already briefly referred to. Here the real business of taking traffic to and from the works was carried on, the yards being connected to the latter by roads known as entrances and labelled for operating convenience with letters of the alphabet, Entrance A, Entrance B and so on. All the works had their own private fleets of shunting engines, and these worked in partnership with the LNER

pilots, accepting loads from the yards as they were brought in and handing over outgoing traffic in the same way, so that the LNER engines never actually entered the works.

Trent Yard was the centrepiece of the original complex, with direct access to the Appleby-Frodingham and Redbourn works, both situated close by. The yard's main function was to handle outward traffic from these works, and for this purpose was split into two groups of sidings known as Top Yard and Low Yard. Like the New Yard, it was connected to the main line at both ends, but a serious drawback was that there was no shunt spur at the western end, which meant that the down goods line had to be used for shunting, resulting in delays to traffic entering the yard as well as holding up the shunting process itself. A further difficulty was experienced at the east end of the yard, where at busy times traffic brought in from the adjacent works by the latter's engines was often deposited in the nearest convenient road, thus conflicting with marshalling processes. Trent Yard required the services of one full-time pilot, working every day except Sunday.

A short distance east of Trent Yard was a smaller yard known as Old Appleby Sidings, serving another part of the Appleby-Frodingham complex, and connected to the main line at one end only. In between the two yards was another small group of sidings at what was known as North Lincoln Junction; it was in this vicinity that incoming trains from the east were dealt with, though the facilities for this were scarcely adequate as there were neither reception roads nor a shunting spur. The procedure was to run trains from the down main line on to the down goods, release the brake-van and then propel back or shunt into North Lincoln or Old Appleby sidings depending on ultimate destination of the wagons involved. The propelling of trains of up to 45 wagons which this required was completely contrary to the regulations, but was the only practical way in which the traffic could be handled. A pilot engine was based at North Lincoln Junction to deal with traffic in both sets of sidings, while the propelling was normally done by the train engine prior to its release for Frodingham Loco.

Totally separate from the rest of the Frodingham network were the sidings at Normanby Park, situated nearly three miles to the northwest and reached via the North Lindsey Light Railway. Comprising 23 roads altogether, these sidings served the Normanby Park works owned by the John Lysaght company. Two Robinson 2-8-0s officiated as pilots, being known locally as 'Lysaghts' Tinies', and one of these also worked as travelling pilot over the twisting and steeply-graded North Lindsey line. The works itself was inhabited by a busy fleet of Peckett tanks which brought loaded steel into the sidings and kept all the works departments well supplied. Traffic for Normanby Park came via the New Yard, except for a few coal trains which ran direct via the North Lindsey west curve.

Besides Normanby Park, the North Lindsey line also gave access to various ironstone sidings, and this traffic was shared between the Normanby Park pilot and private engines belonging to the Appleby-Frodingham company.

From an operating point of view the salient feature of the layout at Frodingham was the large number of trip workings between the various sidings; to make the best use of the facilities, and to gain the fullest advantage from the New Yard, very prompt co-operation was required between the different yards, and it was in this area that, with the gradual growth of traffic, the existing staffing arangements were to be found wanting. Under the original system a single Yardmaster, Mr Barratt, had control of the entire network except for the separate yard at Normanby Park, with over 60 goods guards, 50 to 60 shunters, three inspectors, 11 yard foremen and a number of signalmen all coming under his jurisdiction. The only assistance he received in administering this considerable empire came from a young traffic apprentice, who carried little real authority, and so it is hardly surprising that with developing traffic the Yardmaster became increasingly hard-pressed. The hour-by-hour working of the yard fell on the shift inspectors, but although these were local men who had an intimate knowledge of the Frodingham traffic they did not possess the authority to make the sort of decisions that were often needed at busy times; as their workload continued to grow an assistant yardmaster was introduced, and soon afterwards the arrangement was further amended to provide an assistant yardmaster on each shift. An important part of the assistants' duties was to travel round all the yards in turn, assessing requirements, co-ordinating movements and generally keeping the situation under control; this took the place of a previous system whereby two shunters worked round the yards on each shift, shunting and setting wagons, which had worked well enough as long as traffic was not too heavy. The only slight drawback in the new arrangements was the resentment caused by the decision to bring the new assistant yardmasters in from other parts of the LNER, instead of recruiting them from the local ranks as had been hoped. During these somewhat lean years promotion was not easy to come by. Hence the arrival of the three assistant yardmasters in the spring of 1938, Messrs R. T. Munns and W. Nock from Doncaster, and R. Selley from Lincoln, served only to intensify the local feeling, and must have been an unpleasant

factor for the new arrivals to have to contend with

Normanby Park came under a completel separate dispensation, being superintended by stationmaster whose remit extended as far south a Crosby Mines signalbox on the North Lindsey lin as well as embracing the yard. Staff at the latt consisted of a shunter and numbertaker on eac shift, with three clerks and a number checker o days, the latter responsible for assessing wago demurrage. There was also a Carriage & Wago Department official based at the yard, his tas being to examine the loads of steel leaving th works before giving permission for them to trave on the main line. In earlier LNER days th Normanby Park stationmaster was G. W Mawson, later succeeded by W. Brickell.

As for the enlarged goods yard at Frodingham it was soon fully employed in bringing considerably increased volume of commoditie into the town. As well as the basic necessities, on traffic which grew particularly rapidly was that in bricks; local builders enjoyed an unprecedente boom as new housing estates sprang up, and th situation was faithfully reflected in production a the brickworks owned by the Richard Thoma combine in nearby Crowle, where output ros from a weekly figure of 80,000 bricks during th mid-1920s to 325,000 in 1938, the great bulk of thi being conveyed by the LNER.

The improved goods yard also provide accommodation for the local coal merchants though it did not include one of the district' largest distributors of domestic fuel, the loca Co-operative Society. A separate group of siding capable of taking about 20 wagons was installed a the western end of the New Yard and set aside fo the Society's coal traffic; here empty wagons wer shunted out every evening and fresh ones placed i position for the next day's deliveries. In both th Co-operative sidings and the main goods yard wer to be found the usual variety of private-owner coa wagons so typical of the railway traffic of those years, the red oxides of wagons from such places a Markham, Askern, Thorne, Brodsworth, Hatfiel and Dinnington mingling with the blacks o Frickley, Monk Bretton and Coalite wagons.

A further stimulus to the coal traffic arose from much increased consumption of gas in the district. Opened as late as 1923, Scunthorpe Gasworks had direct access to the North Lindsey line at Dawes Lane.

The years following the opening of Frodingham Loco saw a gradual increase in the number of engines allocated there, as a result of the growth in the production already mentioned, but after the fairly drastic changes described earlier the number of new types introduced into the district was small. Probably the most important development in this direction took place within a few months of the shed being opened when two Class 'L1' 'Crabs' arrived to take up pilot duties; these were Nos 5273 and 5369, both transferred in from Immingham. No doubt the move was also influenced by the trials mentioned earlier. Generally speaking the 'Crabs' had a poor reputation as main-line engines on account of a pronounced tendency to skid when braked, this having resulted in several minor accidents; as a result the management sought to employ them on pilot or banking duties, as at Immingham and Mexborough, and because of the very low speeds required on such duties they were very successful in these roles. They became known amongst the local railwaymen as 'Zeppelins' or 'Zepps', probably because of the Graf Zeppelin airship and its British counterpart the R101 had been so much in the news at the time of their original trials; the nickname may also have harked back to the fact that Frodingham had been bombed by Zeppelins during the Great War as a result of an error of navigation by the German crews. The situation was oddly paralleled at Retford, which had also been accidentally bombed, and where the solitary 'L1' engine rejoiced in the same nickname.

The other locomotive moves of particular interest involved passenger engines. Very little in the way of passenger work had ever been undertaken locally, but in July 1935 a Class D7 4-4-0 arrived from Immingham to take up work on what can safely be described as a fairly rare passenger diagram which appears to have come into currency at about that time. This modest working did not take the engine very far afield, its limits being Barnetby in the east and Thorne in the west, and the rather elderly machines sent to Frodingham to operate it indicate fairly clearly that the work was not of a demanding nature. No 5704 was replaced in September 1936 by another member of the class, No 5708, which by that time was getting due for the scrapheap, and upon its withdrawal the following spring an equally ancient ex-Great Northern engine arrived to take up the duty, 'D3' No 4309, this also being eventually succeeded late in 1938 by a similar machine, 'D2' No 4377. Apart from these comings and goings the only other unusual types to be allocated at Frodingham during these years were former NER and Hull & Barnsley 0-6-0s on temporary transfers into the district. Specimen allocation lists are to be found in the Appendix.

An observer visiting Frodingham shed on the morning of Sunday 1 August 1937 saw a fairly typical collection of locomotives berthed there, consisting in the main of eight-coupled types belonging to Classes O4 and Q4, with Class J11

0-6-0s also well represented. Among the large group of locally based 'O4s' were visitors from Doncaster, Mexborough, Staveley, Immingham, Retford, and Grantham, the last-mentioned having no doubt worked in on one of the regular trains of iron ore from Highdyke[2]. Frodingham used its 'O4s' on a variety of main-line trains as well as the heavy pilot duties mentioned earlier, and the older 'Q4s' acted as a second choice for the main-line workings. The 'J11s' were employed as pilots, being mainly responsible for the frequent trip workings between the yards. Four Class J50 engines were on the shed, including a visitor from Immingham, No 1081, possibly covering for a local engine under repair. Other less usual visitors were an ex-Hull & Barnsley 0-6-0, 'J28' No 2411, 'J6' No 3558 and a 'K2' from Doncaster, No 4633. The remaining engines were Frodingham regulars – the solitary passenger engine, 'D3' No 4309, the two faithful 'Crabs' and the Sentinel, No 172. From the enginemen's point of view it can be said that, generally speaking, the former GCR types were the most popular – the 'O4s' and 'J11s' outstandingly so – while the ex-Great Northern engines were usually disliked; this also applied to the Sentinel, which although it put in many years' service on the Keadby pilot working described earlier, was always regarded with disapproval.

By the date of the shed visit, Frodingham was in the grip of a boom which had had its origins in the noticeable upturn in trade which took place after about 1932. The products which the various steel companies had to offer were coming into increasing demand during these years, and the introduction of Government tariffs on imported steel early in the decade had given business a further boost. John Lysaght's and Redbourn were able to meet a growing market for steel in the automotive, tinplate and electrical trades, the former being one of the leading suppliers of steel to the fast-growing motor car industry, and in 1935 the same firm was able to advertise the use of its wares in the manufacture of the streamlined 'Silver Jubilee' express. The Appleby-Frodingham concern was proud to record the extensive use of its steel girders in major construction projects such as the building of the new Central Library in Manchester.

From the LNER point of view, however, the period was not one of completely unlimited prosperity. Several of their old-established customers in Yorkshire and Derbyshire had been forced to close during the slump, and the ironstone formerly conveyed there from Frodingham now ceased to run. Equally serious were the efforts of certain local firms to seek alternative means of transport, and above all in the plans laid by the John Lysaght company to begin shipping its products from Immingham instead of sending them on the long journey via the GC section to Banbury; the regular steel traffic to their works at Newport in South Wales had operated for so many years that it had long since been taken for granted, and the decision to switch to the much shorter rail route through Immingham must have come as a disagreeable surprise to the LNER management. Nor was this by any means the end of the story, for the switch realised such economies that an even more damaging scheme was promptly put in hand whereby the steel firm set to work to build their own line direct from Normanby Park to the River Trent at Flixborough, whence it could ship steel to Newport without any dependence whatever on outside rail facilities. The LNER thus lost this lucrative traffic entirely once the first shipment had left Flixborough in May 1938.

Some compensation for the various losses was to be found in the increasing commercial viability of certain by-products of the steel industry, the most striking example being that of slag. The discovery that this neglected commodity was in fact an excellent material for road repairing and road making resulted in the growth of a brisk business and brought considerable benefits to the LNER, called on to transport huge quantities of it in connection with road-building projects in various places. Local production of slag was dominated by two concerns, Clugston's and Brookes's, whose highly profitable operations involved nothing more than crushing and grading the slag prior to despatch.

By 1937 there were 10 pilot engines employed at Frodingham, consisting of one in Trent Yard, two **each at North Lincoln sidings and the New Yard, and the remaining five being travelling pilots**

working over the whole network on trip duties. A yards worked round the clock throughout the wee including Saturdays, and the only break in railwa activity was on Sunday afternoons, when the yar inspectors would attempt to 'get squared up' – t use the railway expression – for about 2pm i preparation for the resumption of work at 1 o'clock the same night.

One further improvement was made to th layout about the year 1938 in the building of a ne entry road to the Appleby-Frodingham complex known as Entrance E. Its construction had bee prompted by a southward extension of th Appleby-Frodingham works involving the buildin of new blast furnaces, and was much facilitated b the fact that it followed the route of an ol ironstone railway; the direct connection which i made possible between the New Yard and th works helped considerably towards easing th pressure on Trent Yard and the sidings furthe east. It also afforded room to marshal train coming out of the works and so reduced congestio in Group B sidings at the New Yard.

War came within a short time of the new featur being brought into use, and now it almost seems a though everything that had gone before wa merely a preparation for what was now to come for within a matter of weeks the whole o Frodingham, railway and works alike, was put int top gear to meet the needs of the war effort. Lik so many of the LNER installations, th Frodingham network was to prove its value man times over during the next few years.

Notes
1 George Dow, *Great Central, Vol III*, p 250.
2 Jackson & Russell, *The Great Central in LNER Days,* Chapter 11.

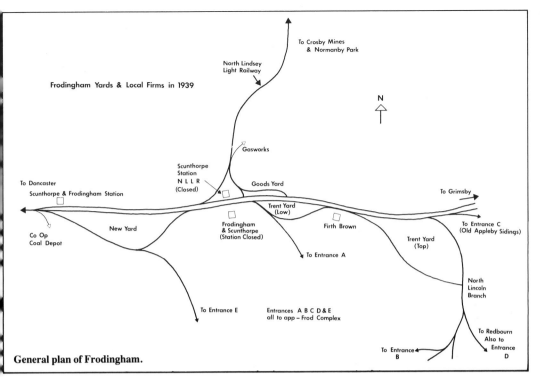

Frodingham Yards & Local Firms in 1939

To Crosby Mines & Normanby Park

North Lindsey Light Railway

N

Gasworks

Scunthorpe Station N L L R (Closed)

Goods Yard

To Doncaster

Scunthorpe & Frodingham Station

To Grimsby

Trent Yard (Low)

New Yard

Frodingham & Scunthorpe (Station Closed)

Firth Brown

To Entrance C (Old Appleby Sidings)

Co Op Coal Depot

Trent Yard (Top)

To Entrance A

North Lincoln Branch

To Entrance E

Entrances A B C D & E all to app – Frod Complex

To Redbourn Also to Entrance D

To Entrance B

General plan of Frodingham.

Left:
Keadby Loco, probably soon after closure.
W. A. Brown collection

Above:
Frodingham in the late 1890s, seen from St John's Church. The Brigg road bisects the main line, with **original passenger station to the left of the level crossing. On the right of the crossing is the second passenger station, with the ornate Station Hotel in between. Beyond the railway is the works of the Frodingham Iron & Steel Co. In the foreground is evidence of opencast mining.**
Scunthorpe Museum

Left:
Usually known as Keadby Bridge, the King George V lifting bridge is in the fully open position in this view looking north. *Authors' collection*

Centre left:
A view from the east bank of the Trent with the lifting bridge open. At the far left tank wagons occupy the incline which formerly led to the original swing bridge. *Authors' collection*

Bottom left:
LNER developments at Frodingham on 12 April 1928. The mile-long diversion from the original main line leads off to the left via a temporary connection adjacent to the original Frodingham & Scunthorpe passenger station, on which work is in progress on cutting back the platform and dismantling the awning. *BR/OPC Railprint*

Below:
'Humpy' and company. An unidentified 0-6-0 saddle tank of a type once common at Frodingham stands at Normanby Park sidings, with Mr Mawson, the stationmaster, wearing a bowler hat, at the centre of the group. *H. Bowdur collection*

Bottom:
'J11' 'Pom-Pom' No 5304 pauses during shunting in 'Winn's Yard', just east of the original passenger station, in 1930. *H. Bowdur collection*

Top:
The new LNER goods depot at Frodingham on 30 July 1929. On the left is the new west curve to the North Lindsey line with the new goods offices beyond. At the centre are the redundant North Lindsey station buildings. The yard is already busy, with most of the siding space taken up. *BR/OPC Railprint*

Above:
Familiar Frodingham traffic. 'O1' No 3475 nears Grantham with ironstone empties on 16 June 1934. *Photo T. G. Hepburn/Rail Archive Stephenson*

Top right:
The Trent Spout at Keadby. A wagon is in the process of

discharging its load, after which it will leave the raised ramp by gravity, its speed controlled by the brake on the cable winding drum. Photographed on 12 April 1933, the apparatus survived well into the BR era. *BR/OPC Railprint*

Centre right:
The new loco shed at Frodingham ready for use, complete with roller-blind doors, and at right there is even a bicycle shed. *W. A. Brown collection*

Right:
Frodingham Loco from the southwest, on 11 August 1932 The Mitchell coal conveyor is in the centre. *BR/OPC Railprint*

KEADBY COAL TIP
TRUCK ON AND TIP LOWERED.
12·4·33. — 4283.

Top:
The eastern end of Frodingham Loco, with water treatment plant in the process of erection.
W. A. Brown collection

Above:
'J50' No 1063 is on the Frodingham Loco turntable on 11 August 1932, with Driver Charlie Mawson and Fireman Ken Jackson officiating as shed shunt crew.
BR/OPC Railprint

Top right:
Eight-coupled mineral engines were always well in

evidence in the Frodingham district. 'O4' No 6287 of Gorton Loco is seen at the shed on 23 May 1937.
Photo W. Leslie Good, per W. T. Stubbs

Centre right:
One of the 'Zeppelins'. 'L1' No 5273 is at Frodingham Loco on 23 May 1937.
Photo W. Leslie Good, per W. T. Stubbs

Right:
Another well-represented mineral type were the 'Q4s'. Here is No 5153 in front of Frodingham Loco on 23 May 1937. *Photo W. Leslie Good, per W. T. Stubbs*

Top:
'D3' No 4309 was sent to Frodingham for passenger work in 1937, and is seen here at the side of the shed on 23 May. *Photo W. Leslie Good, per W. T. Stubbs*

Above:
Railwaymen all: Scunthorpe & Frodingham passenger staff about 1935. Back row, left to right: Archie Corton (porter-guard), Frank Wainwright (booking clerk), Ross Warburton (porter-guard), George Cook (parcels lorry driver), Arthur Bratten (parcels lorry driver), Tom Dawson (parcels lorry driver), ? Ray (porter), J. E. Pickup (porter). Front row, left to right: Sid Lockwood (booking clerk), Ted Thompson (foreman), T. France (stationmaster), J. Herrod (foreman), George Rimington (booking clerk). *Photo Mrs P. Shaw*

Top right:
First shipment of steel out of Flixborough Wharf, on 11 May 1938. The *Eleanor Brooke* has arrived to convey 1,400 tons of steel billets to the company's works at Newport, and sailed two days later. This switch to shipping severely affected the LNER in Frodingham. *Authors' collection*

Right:
Frodingham in 1984, looking south. The Brigg Road overbridge can be seen prominently at the right, and in the foreground is the North Lindsey line, lying at right angles to the main line, which crosses the middle of the picture; the site of Frodingham Loco is in the left foreground. *Grimsby Evening Telegraph*

In Memory

'The number of Great Central men who joined the Colours was 10,190. These included representatives of all the different departments, including that of General Manager, and they were engaged in every branch of His Majesty's service, filling positions from Private to Lieutenant-Colonel.'

Edwin Pratt, *British Railways and the Great War*, *Vol II*,1921

When World War 1 ended on 11 November 1918 after more than four years of the most unrelenting bloodshed the world has ever seen, there quickly followed, in this country and elsewhere, a desire to preserve in some tangible form the memory of those who had made the supreme sacrifice. This sentiment affected the country's railway companies for two special reasons, firstly because many of their employees had left railway service to join the Forces, and secondly because the railways themselves were from the very start in the forefront of the war effort, not only in the movement of troops and materials in this country, but also in the principal war zone itself.

It was therefore natural that some of the first permanent war memorials should appear at passenger stations and goods depots, the result of purely local initiatives among the staffs concerned; the memorials were usually quite simple and unostentatious, normally taking the form of a plaque or tablet bearing the names of the fallen. Two GC section examples which may be mentioned were at Marylebone goods depot and at Mexborough passenger station. The former, sited in the goods depot offices, was dedicated to the members of staff who had lost their lives, and at Mexborough the Locomotive, Traffic and Goods Departments sponsored a joint collection which provided a fine memorial plaque mounted on the wall of the main station building: this is still in position at the time of writing. The Marylebone memorial was transferred to the passenger station following demolition of the former in the BR era.

Superimposed on such local activity came the wish of the companies to commission their own official monuments. These were very much grander, naturally, and were usually sited at the most important passenger stations, where they could act as a reminder to the travelling public of the contribution the companies had made to victory. In this connection it may be mentioned that some of the larger companies, such as the London and North Western and the Midland, had erected earlier memorials to employees killed in the Boer War nearly 20 years before; this however did not apply to the Great Central.

The idea of erecting a permanent monument was carried a stage further by the decision, taken by three of the railway companies, to have a mobile memorial in the shape of a suitably named locomotive; these three were the London & North Western, the London, Brighton & South Coast, and of course the Great Central, whose locomotive forms the principal theme of this chapter. First on the scene with this novel idea was the LNWR, as perhaps befitted a concern which liked to call itself 'The Premier Line', and which specialised in bestowing a great variety of names on its locomotives: a new Claughton Class 4-6-0 emerged from Crewe Works in April 1920 numbered 1914 and bearing the name *Patriot*. The highly symbolic number had already been in use on another locomotive since 1917, but the management had no hesitation in transferring it to the new engine, and a further significant touch was the application of an unadorned matt black livery to the travelling memorial. On the LBSCR the engine chosen to honour the company's fallen was a 4-6-4 tank, numbered 333 and named *Remembrance*. The name had been suggested by Mr C. N. Anderson, a District Traffic Officer on the 'Brighton'. [1]The machine went into service two years after *Patriot*, in the spring of 1922.

The Great Central's mobile memorial belongs chronologically between these two, appearing in July 1920. The fact that it came on the scene so very soon after *Patriot* must inevitably raise some question as to what extent the authorities at Marylebone were influenced by the appearance of the latter, particularly as GCR and LNWR locomotives worked cheek-by-jowl with one another at Manchester London Road, a station which *Patriot* is known to have favoured in its first few weeks of working. It is a very evident and yet little-recorded fact that throughout the long career of John G. Robinson at Gorton the Great Central had shown considerable willingness to copy LNWR ideas when it came to naming, and this even extended in some cases to the use of identical names. As to how or why the GCR came under this singular influence, no definite reason can be given, but it is noticeable that during the poignant years following the war the LNWR made wide use of names associated with the conflict, ranging from the location of battles to a variety of personalities – war leaders, heroic figures such as Captain Fryatt and Edith Cavell, as well as the company's own winners of the Victoria Cross; no doubt many of the engines concerned, like *Patriot*, appeared from time to time at London Road, and so the Great Central may well have felt that not to do something similar might be construed as unpatriotic. Such perhaps was the reasoning behind the emergence of *Valour*, No 1165 of Class 9P, and the resemblance to LNWR practices was much enhanced by the fact that this engine was in appearance, wheel arrangement, tractive effort and function a close match for No 1914.

Both *Patriot* and *Valour* appeared before either company had completed a permanent official memorial, and it is possible that the LNWR and GCR managements may have regarded these engines as a way of giving notice of their intention to construct a more conventional monument in due course. This however was not true of the LBSCR, whose 'Roll of Honour' at London Bridge may be found described in the *Railway Magazine* of 1920, and it may therefore be that the later decision to commission *Remembrance* was influenced by the appearance of the LNWR and GCR engines.

A comparison between the various styles of memorial nameplates is interesting, and although the Great Central may not have initiated the idea of building a memorial engine it may perhaps be claimed that they carried off the honours when it came to designing the plate. Despite its time-honoured use of such a rich variety of names, the LNWR had always kept to a rather austere style of plate, involving a plain strip of rolled brass with simple cut-out letters, and so when it came to producing something special their ideas, we may imagine, were stretched to the limit, particularly as it was the intention to incorporate an inscription below the name. *Patriot* eventually emerged with rather elaborate plates in the form of an elongated cross, but in other respects these adornments reflected the usual Crewe custom, the letters being cut out and filled with black composition, and the edges of the plates innocent of any noticeable border. The letters themselves were plain block capitals, corresponding closely to the usual Crewe style.

By comparison, the plates affixed to *Valour* were among the most striking ever to appear on any locomotive in this country – to see this, the reader is invited to examine the accompanying illustrations. The unusual shape of the plate, intended to represent a shield, and the contrasting styles of script, combined to produce something

very different from the usual GCR nameplate, and it is clear that the draughtsmen had made exceptional efforts to meet the occasion; unfortunately nothing is known of the persons responsible.

Because of the great size of these plates there was no room for the Gorton works plate in the usual position below, and so No 1165 emerged with these mounted on the cylinder covers – another unique touch. Nothing was attempted in the way of special number or livery however, the engine following the sequence for its class and appearing in the usual Brunswick green.

With *Remembrance* the LBSCR adopted a rather different approach. Instead of making use of a nameplate it followed the company's normal custom of painting the name in large, striking characters above a small memorial plaque, and in preference to its usual effulgent passenger livery chose to paint the engine a dull grey, possibly influenced by the example of *Patriot*. Perhaps, if reports of *Valour's* appearance had been conveyed to the LBSCR management, they may have decided that a shiny livery was unsuitable for a memorial locomotive. Under SR auspices however different philosophies soon prevailed, and the engine was repainted malachite green in 1924.

There were some variations in the inscriptions, particularly concerning the dates given. Both the LNWR and LBSCR gave 1914-1919 as the beginning and end of the conflict, whereas the GCR displayed the version which is nowadays more usual – 1914-1918. In a sense, both sets of dates are correct. Although hostilities actually ceased at the 1918 Armistice it was not until the middle of the following year that the Treaty of Versailles officially brought the war to an end. It will also be remembered that during this period Allied troops were in action in Russia, although the loss of life in this short campaign was slight. As to the wording of the inscriptions, it will be noticed from a comparison of the illustrations that the LBSCR chose a form of words closely based on those used on the *Valour* nameplates.

A fourth war memorial engine may be briefly mentioned here. Far away on the other side of the world, four years after the appearance of *Remembrance*, the New Zealand Government Railways staged a ceremony at Dunedin in which a Class AB Pacific was commissioned as the NZGR memorial locomotive. Though these events were greatly separated in space and time from what had taken place at Gorton there was nevertheless an important connection with the latter, for at this period the CME of the New Zealand Railways was a certain G. S. Lynde, who had gone out from the Mother Country shortly before to take up this new position; he had previously worked in the GCR locomotive department at Gorton.

The later history of *Valour* and its British rivals affords something of a contrast. Neither the LNWR nor LBSCR engines lasted for very long in their original form, and there were also changes in the naming style. As a result of the adoption of a definite naming policy on the Southern Railway, *Remembrance* received a nameplate in place of the painted letters in 1926 and then, in connection with certain developments in the locomotive sphere, was rebuilt as 4-6-0 tender engine some years later, in which form it emerged with new crescent nameplates over the centre splashers. As for *Patriot*, the original locomotive and plates disappeared completely from the scene with its withdrawal in 1934, and the name was transferred to a Fowler 4-6-0; completely new nameplates were fitted, of crescent shape and considerably smaller than the originals. In contrast, the nameplates on *Valour* remained untouched; apart from repainting in LNER colours and the fitting of a different style of chimney, the engine was never altered in any way between its entry into traffic and withdrawal 27 years later, and the plates survived intact.

The first Armistice Day in 1919 was observed throughout Britain by two minutes silence at 11am. Whitehall had been designated as the site of a national war memorial, and although the monument itself had not then been completed, large crowds gathered before a plaster replica to take part in the first Service of Remembrance. The intention, clearly, was that 11 November should be observed in the same way each year. During the following year permanent war memorials began to appear, and it is to this period that *Patriot* and *Valour* belong.

On 11 November 1920 *Valour* was diagrammed to work the 8.20am Manchester-Marylebone express, and for this duty it was suitably decorated with wreaths, one round each of the nameplates and another on the smokebox door. Reaching Leicester at the booked time of 10.56, it came off the train in accordance with the normal diagram, and then stood nearby while two minutes silence was observed. Having changed engines, the 8.20 was booked to depart at 11am, but left two minutes late following the silence; rail traffic everywhere was interrupted in this way. *Valour* then proceeded with the return half of its diagram in the normal way, still bearing its distinctive embellishments. It is believed that similar arrangements operated in the following year.

During 1922 the company's permanent war memorial was completed, with Sheffield Victoria chosen as its site. No doubt this was because of the traditionally close associations between the GCR and that city, which of course went right back to the 1840s and the opening of the Woodhead line. Taking the form of a stone Arc de Triomphe, the monument incorporated panels bearing the names of the 1,304 men of the Great Central who had lost their lives on active service. It was placed in a strikingly prominent position directly outside the main station entrance, at right angles to the roadway; clearly visible along the full length of the approach, it added a touch of some distinction to the otherwise rather drab station frontage. It was unveiled on Wednesday 9 August 1922 by no less a personage than Field Marshal Earl Haig. For this great occasion every effort was made to ensure that families and relatives of the deceased should have the opportunity to be present, and special trains were run from Manchester, London and Cleethorpes. Earl Haig travelled to the ceremony in the company of a distinguished gathering of Great Central notables that included Lord Faringdon, Walter Burgh Gair and Sir Sam Fay; the party were conveyed in the directors' saloon, attached to the rear of the 10am Marylebone-Bradford express. The choice of locomotive was a typical piece of GCR showmanship – No 1166 *Earl Haig*, sister engine of *Valour*. The workings are believed to have been specially altered so that instead of engines being changed at Leicester in the normal way, *Earl Haig* worked the train through to Sheffield, with Driver Willoughby Lee at the regulator. Both he and his engine were based at Gorton, and this specially arranged working offers a good example of the way in which Gorton Loco usually managed to get into the limelight on such occasions. The Manchester special was headed by *Valour*, and it is believed that Driver Bill Chapman was in charge.

With the unveiling of the new memorial the stage was set for an annual visit of *Valour* to Sheffield Victoria on 11 November, with nameplates decorated as described earlier, and this pleasing custom was to continue throughout the period between the wars.

Because of its special associations, *Valour* was always regarded with particular pride on the GCR section, but like the rest of Class 9P, or B3 as it became known under the LNER, the locomotive had a somewhat nomadic existence. When first introduced it was based at Gorton and in the hands of a regular driver, Bill Chapman, but soon after Grouping it was transferred away from the GC section altogether, being sent with the other members of its class to the former GNR shed at Kings Cross. It came back to Gorton for a short spell in 1927 and was then sent to Immingham at the end of the following year, as described in an earlier chapter. From then until almost the outbreak of World War 2 it alternated between Immingham and Neasden except for another few months at Gorton in 1934-35; its last move in the peace years took place just a few weeks before World War 2 began, when it was sent from Immingham to Woodford. During all these years, regardless of where it happened to be stationed at the time, it was always released from normal service early in November so that it could return temporarily to Gorton for the Armistice Day ceremony. In this connection it is worthy of note that even in the year 1925, when it was officially under repair in Gorton Works from the last day in October until 14 November, it was still noted as taking part in the memorial ceremony as usual; since its spell in the works was quite short by the standards of those days, it would seem that the works staff made a special effort to carry out the necessary work in time for 11 November. It is probably significant that there are no other instances of it having undergone repairs at this time of year.

Its move to Kings Cross in the summer of 1923 was notable in one respect, namely that in spite of having received a full overhaul at Gorton immediately beforehand, it arrived in London in original GCR livery, without even its new number. Although the ultimate LNER style of painting and lettering had not at this time been finalised, a temporary renumbering scheme was in operation whereby GCR engines received a letter 'C' suffix after the number, and an early form of LNER lettering was being applied in place of the legend 'Great Central'. *Valour* received none of these embellishments, and was either refurbished without being sent to the paint shop, or else was completely repainted in original colours, despite the fact that the GCR had been defunct for nearly eight months. Whatever happened, there can be no doubt that this episode belongs with several other publicity stunts which were indulged in at this time, involving GCR engines allocated to or working over other parts of the LNER. The guiding hand behind all these things, undoubtedly, was that of W. G. P. Maclure. The reluctance to repaint *Valour* at this time, or to alter its external appearance in any way, may also be taken as testimony of the esteem in which it was held at Gorton, particularly at this early period when most of the original GCR management and staff were still to be found there – these included R. A. Thom, W. M. Smith and William Rowland, respectively Assistant to the CME, Works Manager, and Chief Locomotive Draughtsman. All three men would undoubtedly have had a considerable hand in the design of *Valour* and her sister engines.

On the day of the annual ceremony, *Valour* received special attention from one of the Gorton cleaning gangs, and many photographs testify to the immaculate condition in which it was turned out. At Gorton the cleaning of main-line passenger engines was always something of a fetish, being regarded as a valuable means of boosting the shed's prestige, and on any sort of special occasion there was an even greater keenness to produce the desired standard of finish; anything less than the best would be seen as harming the shed's reputation. However, during the spell which *Valour* spent on the GN section it would appear that for at least a part of the time it was not maintained up to the high standard of cleanliness which it would have enjoyed in normal service at Gorton, as there was one occasion when it was sent back for the Armistice Day ceremony in a somewhat neglected condition, and according to a story told by a former Gorton man, Harry Beddoes, a message was sent to Kings Cross requesting that the engine should not be allowed to get into such a state in the future. The reason for its neglect was probably to do with the fact that the class was unpopular at Kings Cross, rather than with any necessary difference in the standards of cleaning at the two sheds.

The Armistice Day ceremony itself, or rather ceremonies, began in Gorton Loco yard, where *Valour* was standing spick and span on its appointed road. Wreaths were placed on each of the nameplates, and sometimes an additional one on the smokebox door, and the engine then set off tender-first for Platform A at London Road where it backed on to its train. In the years from 1922 onwards a small ceremony took place on the platform in which a third wreath was handed to two previously chosen representatives of the Gorton Works staff, who boarded the train and conveyed the wreath to the service at Sheffield Victoria, during which they laid it on the memorial.

To reach Sheffield at the appropriate time, *Valour* normally worked out of Manchester on the 10.03 Cleethorpes express, which gave an arrival at 11.08, shortly after the service had begun. There were however some variations, as for instance when 11 November fell on a Sunday, which happened in 1923, 1928 and 1934. The 10.03 was a weekdays-only departure, and in 1923 there was no train from Manchester giving an arrival in Sheffield at any time near 11 o'clock. By 1928 there was a semi-fast out of London Road at 10.25 which reached Sheffield at 11.35, probably just towards the close of the service. In 1934 this train had been retimed to leave at 10.20, with an arrival in Sheffield at 11.32. *Valour* is reported as having worked the latter in 1934[2], but no details have been traced for the other two Sundays. The 10.20 is believed to have been a Sheffield working in 1934, and so it would appear that special arrangements were made to allow *Valour* to work it on that occasion. Its predecessor the 10.25 was also a Sheffield turn, and it seems probable that similar special workings were put into effect in 1928 to enable *Valour* to make its customary appearance.

Another unusual occasion was 1927, when for some reason which has not been traced, *Valour* worked to Sheffield on the 8.20 Marylebone train, giving an arrival 1½ hours before the ceremony was due to begin. A further curiosity of that year was the fact that photos of the engine and its decorated nameplates were taken and subsequently published in the company's magazine[3]. These events may possibly be explained by the fact that in this particular year the service at Victoria was conducted by the Bishop of Sheffield, instead of the usual celebrant. The 8.20 was again made use of in 1938, but on that occasion the circumstances were somewhat exceptional as the memorial had been removed to make way for extensive reconstruction work which was then taking place; because of this there was no service at the station, and instead the representatives from Gorton took their wreath to the Sheffield Corporation memorial at Barker's Pool, which was some distance away, and which they could not have reached in time had they travelled on the 10.03.

The wreaths placed on the engine nameplates were made of laurel, rather than the poppies usually associated with Remembrance services. The latter came gradually into use following the promotion of 'Poppy Day' by the British Legion, and poppies were usually included in the separate wreath brought from Gorton, but so far as is known they were never used for the nameplate wreaths. All the wreaths were paid for out of voluntary contributions from members of the various departments, and this of course included wreaths brought to Sheffield from other parts of the GCR; at Doncaster for instance the Great Central staff made a separate collection for their own wreath, while their Great Northern colleagues collected at the same time for a wreath to be sent to the memorial at Kings Cross.

The service at Sheffield appears to have followed a more or less regular pattern, no doubt much the same as other Remembrance services elsewhere. The participants assembled at the memorial shortly before 11 o'clock, and the service began after the national two minutes silence; as it did so it was usual for the Cleethorpes express to come steaming into Platform 4 at its appointed time of 11.08, with the appropriately decorated *Valour* at the head. The engine was uncoupled from the train and ran back along the centre road, coming to rest in a spot directly opposite the memorial; at the same time the two Gorton Works representatives made their way to the memorial, taking the wreath with them. The engine remained in its position until the service was over, and then

moved off to resume its diagram. Up to 1927 the return working of the 10.03 was on the down 'Continental', due out of Sheffield at 12.50, and so there was ample time for *Valour* to wait until the end of the service before proceeding to the turntable at Blast Lane, close by the station. By 1929, the next occasion on which *Valour* worked the 10.03, the original diagram had been scrapped as a result of the introduction of lodging on the 'Continental', and the next part of the working took the engine forward to Leicester at 11.37 on a York-Bournemouth express. The 8.20 diagram was also changed as a result of the new Continental turn; until 1927 the Gorton engine had worked as far as Leicester, so that when *Valour* worked its inaugural trip to Leicester in 1920 it was in fact following the normal diagram; when it once again worked the 8.20 in 1927 the new working had come into force whereby engines were changed at Sheffield. These changes in diagramming were part of an extensive revolution in main-line passenger workings brought about by the introduction of the 'Continental' lodging turn, but the full story of these developments lies outside the scope of the present volume, and must await a future occasion to be told.

The two local Sheffield newspaper, the *Telegraph* and *Independent*, regularly reported the Victoria station ceremony, but the latter's item of 1929 is the only one which adds anything to our knowledge of the event from a strictly railway point of view. It reads:

'As the service on No 1 Platform was about to start, the LNE remembrance engine 'Valour' with the name on the front encircled with a large wreath steamed into the station with a train from Manchester. The arrival of the engine, which was driven by an ex-serviceman, Driver Rickards of Gorton, Manchester, was singularly appropriate to the occasion, for it was built especially as a memorial to the employees of the old GCR and LNER who were killed in the war.'

The reporter's ignorance on certain points is very apparent, but the mention of one of Gorton's well-known footplate figures, Jimmy Rickards, adds considerable interest to the account as it hints at a slight change in the manning arrangements. The working of the 10.03am diagram is believed to have been regularly entrusted to crews in Gorton's No 2 Link, but Driver Rickards is understood to have belonged to the Top Link, hence this suggests that the Armistice Day turn, because of its prestige, was handled only by the most senior crews. Though the existence of such an arrangement cannot be definitely confirmed, it would of course have been entirely typical of the way in which things were done at Gorton Loco in those days.

In 1932 the *Sheffield Independent* reported what seems to have been something of a departure from the norm inasmuch as after the ceremony *Valour* was inspected by a party of schoolboys and choristers. The latter were almost certainly from Holy Trinity Church, Wicker, the nearest parish church to Sheffield Victoria; the rector of Holy Trinity, the Rev Frank Yates, regularly officiated at the Remembrance services, and the only occasion on which he is known not to have done so is in 1927, when as mentioned earlier the celebrant was His Lordship the Bishop of Sheffield.

Valour was usually sent to Gorton a few days prior to 11 November in order to be got ready for the Armistice ceremony, probably being replaced at the shed where it was based by an engine sent from Gorton in exchange. Unfortunately no record of this transfer appears to have survived, but there are some notes for the year 1935 which are worth adding to the story. In the autumn of that year *Valour* came to Gorton for the usual periodic repair, being released from the works on 12 October. The usual procedure was for engines fresh out of the works to spend a few days on light running-in turns before being returned to their appropriate sheds; this process usually lasted about a week or 10 days unless difficulties arose necessitating a return visit to the works, which was unusual with engines of Gorton design. On this particular occasion however *Valour* was retained in Manchester from leaving the works until well after Armistice Day, working as though on loan to Gorton during this period. Its first noted appearance on a main-line duty following repair was on Thursday 24 October, when it came into Manchester Central on the 12.17 arrival, a Cleethorpes-Manchester train forming the return working of the Gorton engine which had gone out of London Road with the 8.20am express to Marylebone; this was a regular No 2 Link diagram at that period. In succeeding days *Valour* was observed on other No 2 Link workings, particularly two evening jobs, the 5pm Cleethorpes and the 7.22pm Manchester-Leicester. Its last recorded appearance during its spell at Gorton was on 21 November, when it worked the latter.

By 1935 public interest in the national Armistice Day ceremonies had dwindled considerably, understandably so as the war receded further into the past, and this was reflected in falling attendances at Sheffield, as elsewhere. In 1923 1,000 people are reported to have attended the Great Central service, but by 1937 this had fallen to 300. However, the practice of sending wreaths to Sheffield continued without a break, and there is no doubt that, had World War 2 not altered the shape of things, the annual gathering and associated workings of *Valour* would have

remained a feature of the GC section. A short service was in fact held at the memorial on Armistice Day 1939, although by this date the memorial had been resited in the station booking hall followed the reconstruction work referred to earlier; *Valour* is believed to have been present as usual for this occasion, but as World War 2 gathered momentum there was less and less time or desire to dwell on the dead of an earlier conflict. Once the war was over, things changed rapidly. Badly run-down (as were all the ex-GCR 4-6-0s), *Valour* was never to be restored to her prewar condition and was scrapped at the end of 1947. Despite the fact that there was now a second generation of war dead to commemorate, there was no revival of anything resembling the railway observances of post-1918 and so the ceremony described in this chapter, so typical in many ways of the interwar years, passed into history.

Perhaps it was somehow symbolic of the postwar era of austerity that, following its withdrawal from service, *Valour* stood for some time during the early part of 1948 in the sidings at Dukinfield Works, awaiting the breaker's torch in the company of several other derelict ex-GCR 4-6-0s: the nameplates had been removed, and with exposure to weather the unpainted section of each splasher quickly became bright red with rust, faithfully and somewhat ironically reproducing the unmistakable shield-shaped outline. This woe-begone spectacle was clearly visible from the main line, along which in former times *Valour* had so often worked, resplendent in all the glory of GCR or LNER passenger green.

However, the engine claimed one final distinction – that of being the last of its class to be broken up. The lapse of time between official withdrawal of a locomotive from service and its cutting-up varied considerably, but a study of the GC section records shows that it was rarely more than a year. Taken out of service on 31 December 1947, *Valour* is recorded as having survived intact until 7 January 1950, by which date all its sister engines had gone for scrap, including the rebuilt No 1497 (late No 6166 *Earl Haig*), which had been withdrawn in the autumn of 1948. Whether this exceptional lapse of time points to some possible preservation attempt cannot be stated in the absence of other evidence, but seems the only explanation of what happened – unless it was simply that the authorities at Gorton were reluctant to see the much-respected machine cut to pieces.

One of *Valour*'s nameplates was mounted on the wall at Gorton works, where it remained until the premises were closed in 1963; it was afterwards transferred to the nearby Church of St Barnabas, whence it was stolen and has never since been recovered. The other plate was sent to the York

Railway Museum where it may still be seen at the present time. As for the Victoria station memorial, this was moved for the second time when the station was closed in 1970, and the tablets bearing the roll of honour have since been mounted on one of the pillars of Sheffield's Wicker Arch, over which GCR and LNER trains have so often passed.

The official withdrawal of *Valour* on the last day of December 1947 coincided exactly with the close of the LNER era. In a deeper sense it can be said to have symbolised the fact that the kind of scenes which have been described in this book now belonged totally to history. Though strictly speaking these things had already vanished into the past in September 1939, the engines which contributed so much to them lingered on through

the war, and ironically doing work more vital than they had ever done before. With the return of peace it was a different story, and most of the GCR types were soon to become victims of the LNER postwar plans. *Valour* was not alone in being withdrawn in the postwar era, for with it went every express passenger and fast goods engine that Gorton had ever designed, except for the 'Directors', in a clean sweep that came to its melancholy end in 1950. The disappearance of so many of the old favourites meant that the GCR line could never be quite the same again, and so in a sense the end of *Valour* was the end of so much that has been written about in this book.

Notes
1 O. J. Morris, 'As They Were', *Trains Illustrated* October/November 1949.
2 *LNER Magazine*, December 1934.
3 *LNER Magazine*, December 1927.

Above:
In Memory. *Photo L. Hanson*

Top right:
Staff of the GCR Goods Department at Marylebone commissioned this simple plaque after the Great War. It is unusual in giving the locations where the deceased were killed. *Photo B. Longbone*

Centre right:
Eleven o'clock on Armistice Day 1920, at Leicester

Central. Passengers and railway staff observe the two minutes of silence with hats removed. On the footplate are Driver Bill Chapman and Fireman Sam Butterton of Gorton, with Inspector Harry Bailey of Neasden seen standing by the side of the tender.
C. H. S. Owen collection

Right:
Armistice Day 1923, at Guide Bridge. No 1165 *Valour* is returning to Manchester after the service at Sheffield, with wreath round the nameplate. *Real Photos*

GREAT CENTRAL RAILWAY COMPANY

MCM XIV-XIX

CHIEF GOODS MANAGER'S OFFICE   MARYLEBONE, LONDON.

To the Glorious Memory of our Colleagues
who laid down their lives in the GREAT WAR.

NORMAN H. SMITH.	Q.V.R.	YPRES 21st APRIL 1915.
GEORGE W. SLADE.	Q.V.R.	GUINCHY 9th SEPT. 1916.
HARRY F. SALTER.	Q.V.R.	COMBLES 9th OCT. 1916.
THOMAS V. SCATTERGOOD.	N.F.	MESSINES RIDGE 6th JUNE 1917.
CECIL E. ROSE.	R.I.F.	FRANCE 10th SEPT. 1917.
CLAUDE C. COOK.	RANGERS	YPRES 29th SEPT. 1917.
WILLIAM L. HOWES.	M.G.C.	WYTSCHAETE 16th APRIL 1918.
NORMAN J.W. HELLIWELL.	H.A.C.	PIAVE RIVER 31st OCT. 1918.

"The path of Duty is the way to Glory."

Top:
LNWR memorial engine No 1914 *Patriot* at Crewe North
Loco, painted in unadorned matt black. An Armistice
Day service was regularly held at Rugby Loco, with this
engine participating. *Lens of Sutton*

Above:
No 333 *Remembrance,* the LBSCR memorial engine, is
seen at Battersea shed with regular driver Henry Funnell

at left in the cab. The inscribed tablet below the name
reads 'In Grateful Remembrance of the 532 men of the
LB&SC Rly who Gave Their Lives for Their Country,
1914-1919', the wording being similar to that of *Valour.*
The engine is in fully lined workshop grey, in which it ran
for a time. It worked a special Armistice Day train from
Brighton to London Bridge in 1924, decorated with a
wreath and poppies. *Lens of Sutton*

Top:
The war memorial at Sheffield Victoria, seen in its original position, astride the station approach. It was designed by T. E. Cullcutt. *Sheffield City Libraries*

Above:
The memorial in its later position inside the entrance, pictured in August 1970 after closure of the station. *Sheffield City Works Dept*

Left:
At Mexborough, the Locomotive, Traffic and Goods Departments contributed to their own memorial on the station building. *H. Bowdur collection*

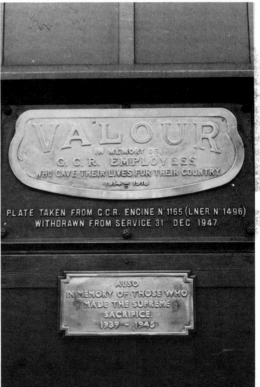

Top left:
An immaculate No 6165 *Valour* seen at Guide Bridge on an eastbound express in the late 1920s. *Real Photos*

Centre left:
The Wicker Arch, Sheffield, in 1952. The GCR memorial tablets were later resited in the small archway visible at right above the car roof. *Sheffield City Works Dept*

Below left:
Wicker Arch on 10 November 1971, with a service of re-dedication taking place; a plaque to mark the transfer from the station was unveiled and a wreath laid.
Sheffield Newspapers Ltd

Above:
In grimy wartime condition, No 6165 *Valour* is seen at Garden Sidings, Doncaster about 1943, with her crew and an apprentice.

Right:
Valour has long since gone, but one of her nameplates remains on view at Gorton Works in this picture of 4 May 1957. *H. Bowdur collection*

Appendices

I Weekday Service, Glossop-Manchester London Road-Glossop, Spring 1935

Depart Glossop Central

am
7.02*
7.35*
8.14*
8.38*
9.55*
11.04*
11.35 change Dinting

pm
12.12 SX
12.18* SO
1.01
1.29*
1.41* SO
2.02 SX
2.25 SO
2.30 change Dinting
3.20 SX
3.50* SO
4.15 change Dinting
4.42 SX
5.10 *
5.20 SO change Godley
5.48 SX change Dinting
6.05 SO
6.15 SX change Dinting
6.52*
8.18*
9.33* SO
10.09
10.56 SO

* Train commences at Hadfield

Depart Manchester London Road

am
5.25 change Dinting
6.40 to Dinting only
8.25*
9.20 change Guide Bridge & Dinting
10.05 change Dinting
10.45* SO
11.08 SX

pm
12.05 SX
12.07 SO to Dinting only
12.27 SO
12.40 SX change Dinting
12.48 SO
1.00 SX
1.25* SO
1.55 SX
2.40 change Dinting
3.29 SX
3.52 change Dinting
4.35*
5.17 SX
5.20 change Dinting
5.55 SX change Dinting
6.31 change Dinting
7.10 change Dinting
8.00* SO
8.25 SX change Dinting
9.00* SO
9.40*
10.10 SO
10.30 SX to Dinting only
11.05 TThsSO to Hadfield SO

* Train continues to Hadfield

126

II Typical Eason's Guaranteed Day Excursions

	8 EP arr. a.m.	8 EP dep. a.m.	10 EP arr. a.m.	10 EP dep. a.m.	12 EP arr. a.m.	12 EP dep. a.m.	14 EP arr. a.m.	14 EP dep. a.m.
Cleethorpes	..	6 55	..	6 55	..	6 51	..	6 55
Grimsby Docks	..	7 3	..	7 3	..	6 59	..	7 3
Grimsby Town	7 6	7 11	7 6	7 11	7 2	7 7	7 6	7 11
Louth	7 30	7 31	7 30	7 31	7 26	7 27	7 30	7 31
Boston	8 11	8 13	8 11	8 13	8 7	8 13	8 11	8 13
Spalding	8 31	8 33	8 31	8 33	8 31	8 33	8 31	8 33
Peterboro' North	8A55	8 59	8 55 A	8 59	8 55 A	8 59	8 55A	8 59
Huntingdon North		9 19		9 19		9 19		9 19
Hitchin		9 47F		9 47F		9 47F		9 47F
Hatfield		10 3H		10 3H		10 3H		10 3H
King's Cross		10C23		10C23		10C23		10C23

	8 EP arr. a.m.	8 EP dep. midt.	10 EP arr. a.m.	10 EP dep. midt.	12 EP arr. a.m.	12 EP dep. midt.	14 EP arr. a.m.	14 EP dep. midt.
King's Cross	..	12 0	..	12 0	..	12 0	..	12 0
Hatfield		12 31J		12 31J		12 31J		12 31J
Hitchin		12 46		12 46		12 46		12 46
Huntingdon North		1 14K		1 14K		1 14K		1 14K
Peterboro' North	1 35	1 39	1 35	1 39	1 35	1 39	1 35	1 39
Spalding	2 1	2 3	2 1	2 3	2 1	2 3	2 1	2 3
Boston	2 20	2 25	2 20	2 25	2 20	2 25	2 20	2 25
Firsby		2 43		2 43	2 45	2 50		2 43
Burgh-le-Marsh	2 46	2 47	..	..	..	..		
Alford Town			..	..	..	..	2 55	2 56
Louth	3 9	3 10	3 7	3 8	3 13	3 14	3 10	3 12
Grimsby Town	3 31	3 38	3 25	3 32	3 32	3 39	3 29	3 36
Grimsby Docks	3 41	3 43	3 35	3 37	3 42	3 44	3 39	3 41
Cleethorpes	3 50	..	3 44	..	3 51	..	3 48	..

A.–M. & G.N. Passenger due 8.55 a.m. to follow.

F.–16 Down C.B. to be kept clear.

H.–269 Up to be turned Slow Line Cemetery, and 282 Up to be kept clear.

J.–864 Down to follow from Welwyn Garden City.

K.–822 Down braked goods to precede this Special through Peterboro' North.

8, STOCK (Vestibuled).–B.T., 5T, 2TO, R.C. P.T. and

10, 12 B.T. Station Master, Cleethorpes, to arrange.
& 14 GUARD.–Station Master, Cleethorpes.

Maud Foster (Boston), High Ferry (Sibsey), Old Leake, Little Steeping, Firsby Station, Burgh-le-Marsh, Willoughby, Alford Town, Aby, Authorpe, Legbourne Road, Louth North, Ludboro', North Thoresby, Holton-le-Clay, Waltham, and Hainton Street (Grimsby) signal boxes to be open for the return train.

16. In Connection with 12 P.S.T.

	A OP arr. a.m.	dep. a.m.	arr. a.m.	dep. a.m.	arr. a.m.	dep. a.m.		B OP arr. a.m.	dep. a.m.	arr. a.m.	dep. a.m.
Skegness	..	7 21	..	..	..	3#23	Boston ..	..	6#20	..	..
Wainfleet	..	7 31	..	2#30	3#33	..	Firsby South	..	6 40	..	..
Firsby South	7 39		..	..	..	..	Firsby Station	..	..	..	2 56
Firsby Station	..	..	2#40	..	..	..	Wainfleet	..	..	..	3 4
Boston	..	7 58	..	..	..	..	Skegness	..	6#55	..	3 13

STOCK.–(Vest.) B.T.. 2T. (To work through).

GUARDS. A.–Goods Agent, Boston.
B.–Station Master, Wainfleet.

Firsby Station, Wainfleet and Skegness signal boxes to be open for these trains.

III Locomotives Allocated to Keadby Shed, 1 January 1923

'O4' 1206, 1240
'Q4' 39, 57, 63, 85, 139, 140, 143, 147, 150, 153, 160, 162, 956, 1074, 1076, 1144, 1178

A rough wooden coaling stage was erected at Frodingham by the LNER, seen still in situ in this 1984 view. In the foreground is the spot where the water column was mounted, this being later transferred to another site in Frodingham. *F. Hallam*

IV Locomotives Allocated to Frodingham Shed, 1 January 1933

'J11' 5216, 5250, 5307, 5315, 5973, 5988, 5995, 6012
'J50' 1058, 1063, 1068, 1072, 1082, 3225
'L1' 5273, 5369
'O4' 5334, 5352, 6215, 6223, 6237, 6242, 6243, 6248, 6250, 6362, 6366, 6515, 6518, 6568, 6569, 6572

'Q4' 5039, 5085, 5139, 5140, 5147, 5150, 5151, 5153, 5164, 5356, 5964, 6074
'Y3' 172

Note: The above lists are not necessarily complete.

A scene in Entrance E about 1939. Standing on the front of 'C4' No 6260 of Frodingham Loco are, left to right, George Clark, (Class One Shunter), Fireman Sid Trafford and Driver Bill Leeman, all local men. The bridge in the background carries the main Brigg Road. *E. Streets*